Insights You Need from
**Harvard
Business
Review**

# RACIAL JUSTICE

# Insights You Need from *Harvard Business Review*

### Business is changing. Will you adapt or be left behind?

Get up to speed and deepen your understanding of the topics that are shaping your company's future with the **Insights You Need from Harvard Business Review series**. Featuring HBR's smartest thinking on fast-moving issues—blockchain, cybersecurity, AI, and more—each book provides the foundational introduction and practical case studies your organization needs to compete today and collects the best research, interviews, and analysis to get it ready for tomorrow.

You can't afford to ignore how these issues will transform the landscape of business and society. The Insights You Need series will help you grasp these critical ideas—and prepare you and your company for the future.

### Books in the series includes:

*Agile*

*Artificial Intelligence*

*Blockchain*

*Climate Change*

*Coronavirus: Leadership and Recovery*

*Customer Data and Privacy*

*Cybersecurity*

*Monopolies and Tech Giants*

*Racial Justice*

*Strategic Analytics*

*The Year in Tech, 2021*

Insights You Need from
**Harvard
Business
Review**

# RACIAL JUSTICE

Harvard Business Review Press
Boston, Massachusetts

Cataloging-in-Publication data is forthcoming.

ISBN: 978-1-64782-112-8
eISBN: 978-1-64782-113-5

# Contents

## Section 2

# How You Can Make a Difference

# Introduction

# PRESSING FOR PROGRESS TOWARD RACIAL EQUITY

by Robert W. Livingston

When I discuss racism with leaders and managers, I like to ask them to imagine being fish in a stream. In that stream, a current exerts force on everything in the water, moving it downstream. That current is analogous to systemic racism. If you do nothing—just float—the current will carry you along with it, whether you're aware of it or not. If you actively discriminate by swimming with the current, you will be propelled faster. In both cases, the current takes you in the same direction. From this perspective, racism has less to do with what's in your heart or mind and more to do with how your actions or inactions amplify or enable the systemic dynamics already in place.

Workplace discrimination often comes from well-educated, well-intentioned, open-minded, kindhearted people who are just floating along, severely underestimating the tug of the prevailing current on their actions, positions, and outcomes. Antiracism requires swimming against that current, like a salmon making its way upstream. It demands much more effort, courage, and determination than simply going with the flow.

But change *is* possible. Intractable as it seems, the problem of racism in the workplace can be effectively addressed with the right information, incentives, and investment. Corporate leaders may not be able to change the world, but they can certainly change *their* world.

I've devoted much of my academic career to the study of diversity, leadership, and social justice, and over the years I've consulted on these topics with scores of *Fortune* 500 companies, federal agencies, nonprofits, and municipalities. Often, these organizations have called me in because they are in crisis and suffering—they just want a quick fix to stop the pain. But that's akin to asking a physician to write a prescription without first understanding the patient's underlying health condition. Organizations and societies alike must resist the impulse to seek immediate relief for the symptoms, and instead focus on the disease. Otherwise they run the risk of a recurring ailment. Effective interventions involve many stages, which I've incorporated into a model I call PRESS—outlined in greater detail in my article "How to Promote Racial Equity in the Workplace" (*Harvard Business Review,* September/October 2020). Here, I offer a very succinct overview.

The stages, which organizations must move through sequentially, are: (1) Problem awareness, (2) Root-cause analysis, (3) Empathy, or level of concern about the problem and the people it afflicts, (4) Strategies for addressing the problem, and (5) Sacrifice, or willingness to invest the time, energy, and resources necessary for strategy implementation. Organizations going through these stages move from understanding the underlying condition, to developing genuine concern, to focusing on correction.

## Problem Awareness

To a lot of people, it may seem obvious that racism continues to oppress people of color. Yet research consistently reveals that on the whole, Whites in the United

States believe that there is more racism against them than against Blacks. (Interestingly, surveys taken since the George Floyd murder indicate an increase in perceptions of systemic racism among Whites. But it's too soon to tell whether those surveys reflect a permanent shift or a temporary uptick in awareness.) These beliefs can undermine an organization's efforts to address racism by weakening support for diversity policies.

Even managers who recognize racism in society often fail to see it in their own organizations or point to their company's commitment to diversity as evidence for the absence of racial discrimination. However, it is important to recognize that even seemingly "race neutral" policies can enable discrimination. Many White people deny the existence of racism against people of color because they assume that racism is defined by deliberate actions motivated by malice and hatred, but racism can occur without conscious awareness or intent. When defined simply as differential evaluation or treatment based solely on race, regardless of intent, racism occurs far more frequently than most White people suspect.

All of this underscore the fact that people's beliefs and biases must be recognized and addressed as the first step toward progress.

## Root-Cause Analysis

Understanding an ailment's roots is critical to choosing the best remedy. Racism can have many psychological sources—cognitive biases, personality characteristics, ideological worldviews, psychological insecurity, perceived threat, or a need for power and ego enhancement. But most racism is the result of structural factors—established laws, institutional practices, and cultural norms. Many of these causes do not involve malicious intent. Nonetheless, managers often misattribute workplace discrimination to the character of individual actors—the so-called bad apples—rather than to broader structural factors. As a result, they roll out trainings to "fix" employees while dedicating relatively little attention to what may be a toxic organizational culture.

Appealing to circumstances beyond one's control is another way to exonerate deeply embedded cultural or institutional practices that are responsible for racial disparities. For example, an oceanographic organization I worked with attributed its lack of racial diversity to an insurmountable pipeline problem, yet it was unaware of entities that could source Black candidates for jobs such as Hampton University, a historically Black college on the Chesapeake Bay, which awards bachelor's degrees in marine and environmental science. Close examination of a *Fortune* 500 company I worked with revealed that the real culprit of its pipeline problem was the culture-based practice of promoting leaders from within the organization—which already had low diversity. Progress requires a deeper diagnosis of the real source of the problems that leaders wish to change.

## Empathy

The next question is whether leaders in the organization care enough to invest the time, resources, and energy into addressing racism. There is a difference between sympathy and empathy. Many White people experience sympathy, or pity, when they witness racism. But what's more likely to lead to action in confronting the problem is empathy—experiencing the same hurt and anger that people of color are feeling.

One way to increase empathy for people of color is through exposure and education. The video of George Floyd's murder exposed people to the ugly reality of racism in a visceral, protracted, and undeniable way. What best prompts people in an organization to register concern about racism in their midst, I've found, are the moments when their non-White coworkers share vivid, detailed accounts of the negative impact that racism has on their lives. Managers can raise awareness and empathy through psychologically safe listening sessions, supplemented by education and experiences that provide historical and scientific evidence of the persistence of racism.

## Strategy

After the foundation has been laid, it's finally time for the "what do we do about it" stage. Most actionable strategies for change address three distinct but interconnected categories: personal attitudes, informal cultural norms, and formal institutional policies.

To most effectively combat discrimination in the workplace, leaders should consider how they can run interventions on all three of these fronts simultaneously. Focusing only on one is likely to be ineffective and could even backfire. For example, implementing institutional diversity policies without any attempt to create buy-in from employees is likely to produce a backlash. Likewise, focusing just on changing attitudes without also establishing institutional policies that hold people accountable for their decisions and actions may generate little behavioral change among those who don't agree with the policies. Establishing an antiracist organizational culture, tied to core values and modeled by behavior from the CEO and other top leaders at the company, can influence both individual attitudes and institutional policies.

## Sacrifice

Although nothing worth having is completely free, racial equity often costs less than people may assume. Seemingly conflicting goals or competing commitments are often relatively easy to reconcile—once the underlying assumptions have been identified.

The assumptions of sacrifice have enormous implications for the hiring and promotion of diverse talent, for at least two reasons. First, people often assume that increasing diversity means sacrificing principles of fairness and merit, because it requires giving "special" favors to people of color rather than treating everyone the same. In reality, fairness requires treating people *equitably*— which may entail treating people differently but in a way that makes sense. (To be clear, different treatment is not the same as "special" treatment—the latter is tied to favoritism, not equity.)

Of course, what is "sensible" depends on the context and the perceiver. Does it make sense for someone with a physical disability to have a parking space closer to a building? Is it fair for new parents to have six weeks of paid leave to be able to care for their baby? My answer is yes to these questions, but not everyone will agree. Equity presents a greater challenge to gaining consensus than equality. Leaders must have the courage to make difficult or controversial calls.

The second assumption many people have is that increasing diversity requires sacrificing high quality and standards. But it's important to understand that quality is difficult to measure with precision. There is no test, instrument, survey, or interviewing technique that will enable you to invariably predict who the "best candidate" will be. Research has found that candidate quality is better reflected by "statistical bands" rather than a strict rank ordering. "Sacrifice" may actually involve giving up very little. Managers should focus on hiring well-qualified people who show good promise, and then they should invest time, effort, and resources into helping them reach their potential.

· · ·

There are a number of ways to respond to racism: You can join in and add to the injury, ignore it and mind your own business, or experience sympathy and bake cookies for the victim. Or, instead, you can experience empathic outrage and take measures to promote equal justice. If you're reading this book, I hope you are making a commitment to doing just this, and the eight articles in *Racial Justice: The Insights You Need from Harvard Business Review* can help. Covering topics ranging from revamping the role of the chief diversity officer, to using people analytics to gain insights on equity problems at your organization, to finding the courage to speak up about racial injustice at work, these pieces provide dozens of research-based approaches you can use to put the PRESS model into action. Many of the articles focus on specific hurdles that Black Americans face in the workplace, while others deal with bias and diversity more generally. They include the experiences of people of color, as well as strategies for Whites to be better allies. Each piece provides universal takeaways for any reader devoted to taking an active role in fighting racism at work.

The tragedies and protests we have witnessed recently have increased public awareness and concern about racism as a persistent problem in our society. The question we now must confront is whether we are willing to do the hard work necessary to change widespread attitudes, assumptions, policies, and practices. Unlike society at large, the workplace very often requires contact and cooperation among people from different racial, ethnic, and cultural backgrounds. Therefore, leaders should host open and candid conversations about how their organizations are doing at each of the five stages of the model—and use their power to *press* for profound and perennial progress toward the goal of reaching racial equity.

# Section 1

# COMPANIES MUST STEP UP

# U.S. BUSINESSES MUST TAKE MEANINGFUL ACTION AGAINST RACISM

by Laura Morgan Roberts and Ella F. Washington

*Editor's Note: We have chosen to include this article unedited from how it first appeared on June 1, 2020, a week after the murder of George Floyd, to better capture the urgency of its call to action and the moment in which it was written.*

T he United States is in crisis. As we write this article, videos of racial violence and racist threats toward Black people in America flood social and news media channels. Public demonstrations against injustice are happening in at least 30 localities. During nonviolent protests, other parties have engaged in vandalism and looting, spurring varied and often disproportionate police response. Several cities are burning, while Covid-19 continues to rage throughout the country, hitting minority communities the hardest.

In a week that focused on "reopening the economy," everyone has become keenly aware that there is more than one pandemic affecting U.S. lives and local economies. As the American Psychological Association has declared, "we are living in a racism pandemic" too. World leaders are weighing in. The United Nations has urged action from U.S. authorities.

No matter your racial, political, or other identity, these events are almost impossible to escape. In particular, millions of Black people and their allies are hurting. And these issues are not ones that organizations or their leaders—from CEOs at the top of the hierarchy to team managers on the frontline—can ignore.

While conventional diversity, equity, and inclusion initiatives focus on employee engagement and belonging, today's challenges reach far beyond marginalization in the workplace. We now see and hear Black people who are suffering from the weight of dehumanizing injustice and the open wound of racism that has been festering for centuries. Black leaders like Robert Sellers, the University of Michigan's vice provost for equity and inclusion and chief diversity officer, are openly sharing their feelings of exasperation. Blogs like Danielle Cadet's caution readers that "Your black colleagues may look like they're okay—chances are they're not." Another social media message that has gone viral really struck us: "There are black men and women in Zoom meetings maintaining 'professionalism,' biting their tongues, holding back tears and swallowing rage, while we endure attacks from a pandemic and police. Understand and be mindful."

The psychological impact of these public events—and the way it carries over into the workplace—cannot be overstated. Research shows that how organizations respond to large-scale, diversity-related events that receive significant media attention can either help employees feel psychologically safe or contribute to racial identity threat and mistrust of institutions of authority.[1] Without adequate support, minority employees are likely to perceive their environments as more interpersonally and institutionally biased against them. Leaders seeking to create an inclusive environment for everyone must find ways to address these topics.

## Avoiding Missteps

First, we'd like to outline three common missteps to avoid.

### Keeping silent

For people not directly impacted by these events, the default response is often silence. Many whites avoid talking about race because they fear being seen as prejudiced, so they adopt strategic colorblindness instead. We know that many managers also think they lack the skills to have difficult conversations around differences.

But no one has the perfect words to address atrocities in our society. It is the leader's responsibility to try, conveying care and concern for all employees but especially targeted groups. As Desmond Tutu once said, "If you are neutral in the situations of injustice, you have chosen the side of the oppressor." You might be tempted to rest on the laurels of your organization's diversity statements and active employee resource groups. But that is not enough. The words of Dr. Martin Luther King remind us: "In the end, we will remember not the words of our enemies, but the silence of our friends."

## Becoming overly defensive

Another common misstep when approaching uncomfortable conversations about racial injustice is to react defensively, especially when our worldviews, positions, or advantages are questioned or challenged. Robin DiAngelo's research on white fragility highlights this phenomenon. For instance, when learning about police brutality against unarmed Black people, one reaction might be to search for evidence about what the victim did to deserve abuse, rather than demonstrating compassion and empathy. Another example is diminishing protesters by focusing on and judging those who engaged in looting instead of discussing the unjust act that drove people to the streets. Leaders must resist such reactions because they do not allow for constructive engagement. Instead, they make members of targeted groups feel even more alienated. Remember that comments on systemic inequalities are not personal attacks.

## Overgeneralizing

When triggering events occur, there is a tendency to make sweeping generalizations about groups of people involved in the public conflict. Though individuals of the same race, gender, or other identity often have shared experiences, there is diversity within groups that should be recognized. Instead of presuming that all members of your in-group or out-group think and feel similarly and talking about what "everybody knows," how "all of us feel," and what "none of us would ever do," leave room for dissenting points of view. When in doubt, ask employees about their individual experiences to honor their uniqueness. Think about how you can allow your employees to discuss what's happening without putting them on the spot or asking them to speak for everyone in their identity group.

Best Buy's senior leadership team offered one of the first corporate statements acknowledging the death of George Floyd under a white police officer's knee in Minnesota, the harassment of bird-watcher Christian Cooper by a white woman in New York City, and the death of jogger Ahmaud Arbery at the hands of armed white gunmen in Georgia, while also paying service to the fact that the Black experience in America is not monolithic: "We write about these . . . events . . . not because most of us know what this fear must be like. We are as a group, by and large, not people of color. We write this not because most of us have known anyone personally in a situation like this. Thankfully, most of us do not. We write this because it could have been any one of our friends or colleagues at Best Buy, or in our personal lives, lying on the ground, struggling to breathe or filming someone as they threatened us."

Citigroup CEO Mike Corbat acknowledged that many employees have experienced racism in their everyday lives in overt and subtle ways. "I want you to know that your colleagues and I will always stand with you," he said in a memo to employees. "While I can try to empathize with what it must be like to be a black person in America, I haven't walked in those shoes."

## Taking Meaningful Action

Next, we'd like to provide a framework for meaningful action. Leaders must not only offer physical and psychological safety. They also have the power and platform to lead change. Statements from the top are valuable, but they are just a start. Anyone, at any level of the organization, can take small steps to exercise greater compassion and initiate action that provides needed support and promotes racial justice for Black workers as well as others who are marginalized. Managers have a particularly important role in connecting with their employees on these issues. Here's how:

## Acknowledge

It's important to acknowledge any harm that your Black and brown coworkers have endured. This means committing to lifelong learning about racism. Seek the facts about racist events, as well as the aggressions and microaggressions that your minority coworkers have most likely faced inside and outside of your organization. We suggest the following steps:

- *Do* the research to fully understand events, using data from reliable sources. Take the initiative to search beyond social media.

- *Do* give your Black and brown employees the space to be angry, afraid, disenchanted, or even disengaged from work.

- *Do* seek out support from your human resources team or office of diversity and inclusion. Books and articles can also be good resources. Three we recommend are: *Race, Work, and Leadership: New Perspectives on the Black Experience,* which one of us edited and to which we both contributed; as well as the related HBR article series "Toward a Racially Just Workplace"; *The Person You Mean to*

*Be* by Dolly Chugh; and *How to Be an Antiracist* by Ibram X. Kendi. There are also free resources such as the "Talking about Race" web portal from the Smithsonian National Museum of African American History and Culture.

- *Do not* rely on Black and brown people to educate you about what happened in order to justify their hurt and outrage or counter "colorblind" rhetoric.

- *Do not* ask your Black and brown leaders or employees to comfort or advocate for colleagues or justice initiatives.

In the organizational setting, you have the power to step up. JPMorgan CEO Jamie Dimon and the company's diversity chief Brian Lamb wrote a memo to U.S. employees stating: "This week's terrible events in Minneapolis, together with too many others occurring around our country, are tragic and heartbreaking. Let us be clear— we are watching, listening and want every single one of you to know we are committed to fighting against racism and discrimination wherever and however it exists."

At Georgetown University, president John DeGioia wrote a heartfelt message to the community acknowledging the harm of a series of racist events: "On too many occasions over the years, there has been cause for me to share reflections with our community, as we grapple with the devastating impact of racism and hatred in our nation. In August 2014, following the killing of Michael Brown in Ferguson, Missouri; in December 2015, following the grand jury decision in the killing of Eric Garner in Staten Island, New York; in August 2017, following the march of white supremacists and neo-Nazis in Charlottesville, Virginia. In these moments, which encompass far from the full extent of experiences of racism and racist violence, I have tried to frame the work in which we must engage within the mission and purpose of the Academy."

## Affirm

People are looking for leaders to affirm their right to safety and personhood and help them feel protected. When presidents, governors, mayors, and sheriffs aren't doing so, corporate, university, and nonprofit leaders can. This means offering continued opportunities for reaction, reflection, conversation, growth, development, impact, and advancement. Affirmation can start with creating a space for employees to share. For example, when asked, "How are you today?" many people of color respond in a scripted manner, instead of answering honestly. Instead, use more thoughtful prompts and questions.

You might say something like this: "I've been thinking about the harm of racism in our country, especially considering recent events." Next, describe your personal reaction and concerns, then make a commitment. "I'd like to help in promoting equity, so here's one thing I plan to do to help prevent future tragedies like these." Explain those intentions. Then, offer to engage. "Please let me know if there's anything else I can do to be supportive, even if you just want to talk about what's happening. I understand if you don't, and I won't be offended. But I just want you to know that the door is open, and that I care." The last line is important. Not everyone will be interested in or comfortable with discussing racism at work, especially if they haven't built a solid foundation of trust.

## Act

Think critically about how you can use your power to effect change. Employees value words of understanding and encouragement, but leaders' and organizations' actions have a more lasting impact. We have witnessed some courageous steps, such as Joan Gabel, president of the University of Minnesota, ending contracts with the Minneapolis Police Department after George Floyd's death. Franklin Templeton Investments fired executive employee Amy Cooper after her interaction with Chris Cooper in Central Park.

Georgetown president John DeGioia's statement went on to say: "Our role in society—to pursue the truth—through the methodologies and disciplines through which we establish knowledge in our world, demands our engagement. In our response, we have sought to accelerate our academic commitment to addressing racial justice and to address our own connection to the institution of slavery and the enduring legacy of racism and to undo the structural elements that sustain this legacy."

More examples include YouTube pledging $1 million to the Center for Policing Equity, Glossier giving $500,000 to support racial justice organizations and another $500,000 to Black-owned beauty brands, and Peloton not only donating $500,000 to the NAACP but also calling for its members to speak up for and learn ways to practice antiracism.

What can you and your organization do in your community? What would promote equity and justice and activate meaningful change? Whether you are a senior or junior leader, how can you advocate for such action?

Racism isn't just Black people's problem; it's everyone's problem, because it erodes the fabric of society. Leaders at every level must use their power, platforms, and resources to help employees and communities overcome these challenges and build a better world for us all.

**TAKEAWAYS**

Leaders at every level must use their power, platforms, and resources to help organizations overcome racism and build a better world for us all. To make meaningful change, avoid three missteps and take three actions:

- ✓ **Don't keep silent** to avoid difficult conversations. No one has the perfect words to address the atrocities in our society, yet it is our responsibility to try.

- ✓ **Avoid becoming overly defensive** when your worldviews, positions, or advantages are challenged.

- ✓ **Refrain from overgeneralizing** about individuals of a particular race, gender, or identity. They may have shared experiences, but there is diversity within groups.

✓ **Acknowledge** any harm that your Black and brown coworkers have endured. Commit to lifelong learning about racism.

✓ **Affirm** your employees' right to safety and personhood. Help them feel supported and protected.

✓ **Act** by using your power to advance racial justice. This could mean enacting policies, pledging money, or organizing in the community.

## NOTES

1. Angelia Leigh and Shimul Melwani, "#BlackEmployeesMatter: Mega-Threats, Identity Fusion, and Enacting Positive Deviance in Organizations," *Academy of Management Review* 44, no. 3 (July 2019): https://journals.aom.org/doi/full/10.5465/amr.2017 .0127; and Alison V. Hall, Erika V. Hall, and Jamie L. Perry, "Black and Blue: Exploring Racial Bias and Law Enforcement in the Killings of Unarmed Black Male Civilians," *American Psychologist* 73, no. 3 (April 2016): https://pubmed.ncbi.nlm.nih.gov/27042881/.

*Adapted from "U.S. Businesses Must Take Meaningful Action Against Racism," on hbr.org, June 1, 2020 (product #H05O6E).*

## 2

# THE 10 COMMITMENTS COMPANIES MUST MAKE TO ADVANCE RACIAL JUSTICE

by Mark R. Kramer

I n the wake of the killing of George Floyd in Minneapolis, many major corporations are tweeting out statements of concern and support for the Black community. That's a start, but what is needed at this moment is action. We cannot pretend that most major corporations in America—and their shareholders—have not benefited from the structural racism, intentional inequality, and indifference to suffering that is behind the current protests. Corporate America and the Business Roundtable have an obligation to go beyond tweets and quotes by committing to an agenda that will advance racial equity in meaningful ways.

Some changes cost virtually nothing; others may create short-term costs. But solid research has shown that the changes that do cost money actually create shared value and lead to both greater long-term corporate profitability and a more prosperous, equitable, and sustainable society. Now is the time to reset expectations for a new and better "normal" to which we can eventually return. Here are 10 commitments that corporations can and should make that will help achieve racial equity.

## 1. Commit to Antiracism Personnel Policies and Racial Equity Training.

Adopt a no-tolerance-for-racism policy like Franklin Templeton's, which led to its swift, recent termination of Amy Cooper following her altercation with Christian Cooper, an African American bird-watcher, in Central Park in New York City. And to back those policies, provide racial equity training for all employees—from the

CEO and board to hourly workers. White privilege has blinded so many of us to understanding the ways that racism is built into our society, our economy, and our own lives. Change, for each of us, must start with our own learning journey, and resources are plentiful.

## 2. Commit to Pay Equity.

There is no longer any excuse for disparities in the wages paid to people of color and especially to women of color whose pay is twice discounted. Conduct a wage equity audit, and make the adjustments needed to achieve fair and equitable pay. For example, PayPal makes adjustments regularly throughout the year to maintain equity. Studies have shown that closing the racial pay gap would increase U.S. GDP by 14%, or more than $2 trillion.[1]

## 3. Commit to Giving Employees a Voice.

Ensure representation of hourly employees, women, and people of color in all employment policy decisions. Consider employee representation on your board—it's a legal requirement in Germany and is one reason why its economy recovered more strongly from the Great Recession than America's and has weathered the Covid-19 pandemic so far with only 4% unemployment.

## 4. Commit to Supporting Full Participation in Democracy.

Make Election Day a paid holiday. Help your employees register to vote by registering them at work.

## 5. Commit to Lobbying for Good.

It is no secret that corporate lobbying shapes many of our laws. Commit at least 50% of your lobbying expenditures to drafting and supporting bills that would improve conditions for communities of color by increasing access to quality education and training, rebuilding infrastructure, protecting consumers, ending racial oppression, rebuilding the safety net, achieving criminal justice reform, and making police more accountable. Remember always that it is the people most deeply affected by these deficits who can best define the problems and necessary solutions. And if your business model relies on immigrants who live, work, and pay taxes in the United States, you owe it to them to stand up for their rights and support a path to citizenship.

## 6. Commit to Paying a Living Wage.

The national minimum wage hasn't been raised in a decade and has not nearly kept up with inflation. This has had a disproportionately negative impact on Black workers, who must routinely hold multiple jobs just to survive. States that have raised minimum wages to $15 an hour have seen their economies grow and thrive.[2]

It's not as expensive as you might think. Research has shown that the companies that pay well and offer good benefits and treat their hourly employees with respect are more profitable.[3] Walmart raised entry-level worker wages to $12 an hour and saw productivity rise while turnover fell, generating a net increase in corporate earnings.

Eliminate last-minute variable shift scheduling that denies employees a 40-hour workweek and disrupts their lives. The Gap found store sales increased 7% when it instituted stable scheduling with two weeks of advance notice.

## 7. Commit to Paid Parental and Sick Leave.

Most women of color cannot afford to take significant periods of unpaid leave from their jobs when they have a child. Given what we know about the critically important role maternal bonding plays in shaping brain architecture and establishing childhood well-being in the first years of life, it's clear that the lack of maternal care has lifelong consequences. The absence of paid sick leave is an even larger problem and one of the reasons people of color have been disproportionately exposed to Covid-19. Providing paid parental and sick leave to all employees can help businesses support thriving and productive workforces.

## 8. Commit to Full Health Care Coverage for All Employees and Support National Health Care.

Corporations spend twice as much providing employees with health care as they pay in taxes. It puts U.S. businesses at a massive global competitive disadvantage, consumes money that might have gone to higher wages, and is causing employers to offload more health care costs on employees. As a result, the take-home pay of people fortunate enough to have employer-sponsored coverage is much less.

Ensure that living wage actually ends up in employees' pockets by reducing their contribution and supporting national health care coverage that would reduce the burden on corporations and would ensure that those without insurance—many of them people of color—are covered. Covid-19, which has disproportionately killed Black and Latinx workers, has underscored the need for equity and universal coverage in health care.

## 9. Commit to an Employee Emergency Relief Fund or Low-Cost Loan Program.

Nearly 40% of Americans—disproportionately people of color—lack the savings to cover even a $400 emergency expense. And that was before Covid-19 destroyed the fragile economic balance that millions of employees struggle to maintain. Their only recourse is to turn to extortionist payday lenders or to run up high-interest credit-card debt.

When there is an emergency, a few hundred dollars advanced by the employer can be life-changing for employees. In addition, consider paying wages weekly instead of biweekly—many employees cannot last two weeks between paychecks—or use PayActiv, which enables employees to access money they have earned before payday.

## 10. Commit to Democratize Employment Applications.

Eliminate the box for "felony conviction" on job application forms, which disproportionately excludes people of color. Eliminate testing for marijuana use and other drugs if not required by law or the nature of the job. Join the companies such as EY, Google, and Whole Foods that no longer require a college degree for jobs that do not actually need higher education. Develop programs to hire, train, mentor, and advance Black youth without high school degrees who face the highest rates of unemployment, yet have been proven to be productive and loyal employees when supported through effective management programs such as those documented by Talent Rewire.

These commitments won't eliminate structural racism, quell protests, or stop continued violence against the Black community, but they are changes within the power of every company that will make a profound difference. These 10 potent commitments could make our companies more profitable, grow our economy, profoundly transform millions of lives for the better, and lead us to become a more equitable, resilient, and prosperous nation. Any one of them will make a difference. How many commitments can your company make?

**TAKEAWAYS**

Major corporations have been voicing their support for racial justice, but words alone do not suffice. Companies should make concrete commitments to achieving racial equity in their workplaces and society. These 10 are within the power of every company:

1. Commit to antiracism personnel policies and racial equity training.

2. Commit to pay equity.

3. Commit to giving employees a voice.

4. Commit to supporting full participation in democracy.

5. Commit to lobbying for good.

6. Commit to paying a living wage.

7. Commit to paid parental and sick leave.

8. Commit to full health care coverage for all employees and support national health care.

9. Commit to an employee emergency relief fund or low-cost loan program.

10. Commit to democratize employment applications.

## NOTES

1. Sarah Treuhauft, Justin Scoggins, and Jennifer Tran, "The Equity Solution: Racial Inclusion Is Key to Growing a Strong New Economy," *Policy Link*, October 22, 2014, https://www.policylink.org/sites/default/files/Equity_Solution_Brief.pdf.

2. Kate Bahn and Will McGrew, "Factsheet: Minimum Wage Increases Are Good for U.S. Workers and the U.S. Economy," Washington Center for Equitable Growth, July 8, 2019, https://equitablegrowth.org/factsheet-minimum-wage-increases-are-good-for-u-s-workers-and-the-u-s-economy/.

3. Zeynep Ton, "The Case for Good Jobs," *Harvard Business Review*, July 2020, https://hbr.org/cover-story/2017/11/the-case-for-good-jobs.

*Adapted from "The 10 Commitments Companies Must Make to Advance Racial Justice," on hbr.org, June 4, 2020 (product #H05OIB).*

# 3

# TOWARD A RACIALLY JUST WORKPLACE

by Laura Morgan Roberts and Anthony J. Mayo

*"Success is to be measured not so much by the position that one has reached in life as by the obstacles which [one] has overcome while trying to succeed."*

Booker T. Washington, the educator, author, activist, and presidential adviser, wrote those words more than a century ago as a way of encouraging his African American compatriots—many of them recently emancipated from slavery—to persist in the fight for equal rights and economic opportunities. He was proud of what he and his peers had achieved. He surely believed there was satisfaction in struggling against and surmounting bad odds. And yet we must also assume that he, along with millions of other freedom fighters, wanted future generations of Black Americans to suffer fewer hardships. He hoped today's Black leaders would find easier paths to success.

Has that dream been realized? Having spent the past 20 years conducting and reviewing research on African Americans' advancement, particularly in the workplace, and having collected our work and others' into a book (*Race, Work, and Leadership*, which we coedited with David A. Thomas), we must report that the answer is partly yes but mostly no.

No doubt, there has been progress. Civil rights laws have been passed and affirmed. Companies are committing to and investing heavily in diversity, because more corporate leaders acknowledge that it makes good business sense. And several Black billionaires and CEOs sit on the respective ranking lists.

However, according to both quantitative and qualitative data, working African Americans—from those laboring in factories and on shop floors to those setting C-suite strategy—still face obstacles to advancement that other minorities and white women don't. They are less likely than their white peers to be hired, developed, and promoted. And their lived experience at work is demonstrably worse even than that of other people of color.

These challenges might, as Washington said, make success sweeter for the few who overcome them. But a huge gap remains between what organizations are saying and doing to promote inclusion and the outcomes we're seeing for many Black workers and managers. If leaders want to walk their talk, they must spearhead much more meaningful change. Instead of undervaluing and squandering Black talent, they must recognize the resilience, robust sense of self, and growth mindset that, studies show, African American people—as one of the most historically oppressed groups in the United States—bring to the table.[1] They should work even harder to seek out and support them, from entry-level recruitment to CEO succession.

We have not identified any major company that is doing this well on a broad scale. But research and lessons gleaned from other contexts can point the way forward. In our work with leading management thinkers and practitioners across the country, we have arrived at a four-step strategy to help companies move toward greater and better representation for Black leaders. It involves shifting from an exclusive focus on the business case for racial diversity to embracing the moral one, promoting real conversations about race, revamping diversity and inclusion programs, and better managing career development at every stage. Given the increasing importance of purpose and social impact to employees, customers, and other stakeholders, we believe there's no better time to make this transformation. We also believe our framework can be adapted for other marginalized groups in the United States and around the world.

Taking these steps won't be easy; executives will need to think deeply about their ethics and corporate culture and exert extra effort for a cause they may not consider central to their business. But the reward will be great: maximizing the human potential of everyone in the workplace.

## Underrepresented, Unsupported, and Unfulfilled

At most large U.S. and multinational organizations, diversity and inclusion (D&I) has become an imperative. Companies are pushing for minority recruitment, paying for antibias training, and sponsoring nonwhite employees for high-potential leadership-development programs. Research has shown, and a great many executives now understand, that a heterogeneous workforce yields more innovation and better performance than a homogeneous one does.[2]

And yet 55 years after the passage of the Civil Rights Act and decades into these corporate D&I efforts, African Americans' progress toward top management roles and greater economic well being and influence remains slow to nonexistent. Let's look first at the demographics.

## What the numbers say

Yes, we can point to the rise of several prominent Black leaders, from media figures Oprah Winfrey, Robert Johnson, and Jay-Z to financiers Ken Chenault and Robert Smith and sports-stars-turned-businesspeople Serena Williams, Michael Jordan, and LeBron James. Most notably, America elected its first African-descended president, Barack Obama, in 2008 and reelected him in 2012. The number of African Americans earning bachelor's and graduate degrees continues to increase.[3] And Black people account for 12% of the U.S. workforce, close to their 13.4% representation in the general population.

However, in the words of leaders from the Toigo Foundation, a career advancement organization for underrepresented groups, such evidence merely gives us "the illusion of inclusion." In fact, research shows that in the United States, the wealth gap between Blacks and others continues to widen; experts predict that Black families' median wealth will decrease to $0 by 2050, while that of white families will exceed $100,000.[4] Just 8% of managers and 3.8% of CEOs are Black. In the *Fortune* 500 companies, there are currently only three Black chief executives, down from a high of 12 in 2002. And at the 16 *Fortune* 500 companies that report detailed demographic data on senior executives and board members, white men account for 85% of those roles.[5]

Black leaders have struggled to make inroads in a variety of influential industries and sectors. At U.S. finance companies, only 2.4% of executive committee members, 1.4% of managing directors, and 1.4% of senior portfolio managers are Black. A mere 1.9% of tech executives and 5.3% of tech professionals are African American. Black representatives and senators account for 9% of the U.S. Congress. The average Black partnership rate at U.S. law firms from 2005 to 2016 was 1.8%. Only 7% of U.S. higher education administrators and 8% of nonprofit leaders are Black. And just 10% of U.S. businesses are owned by Black men and women. As the Toigo Foundation points out, all this has a cascading impact on economic development, housing, jobs, quality of schools and other services, access to education, infrastructure spending, consumer credit, retirement savings, and more.

## What it's like at work

Underrepresentation is bad enough. But even worse, according to extensive research, is the lived experience of Black employees and managers in the U.S. workplace. African Americans continue to face both explicit racism—

stoked by the rise of white nationalism in the past few years—and subtle racism on the job. In the latter category, University of Utah professor emeritus Arthur Brief points to "aversive" racism (when people avoid those of different races or change their behavior around them) along with "modern" racism (when people believe that because Blacks can now compete in the marketplace, they no longer face discrimination).[6] Microaggressions—for example, when a white male visitor to an office assumes that a Black female executive is a secretary—are also common.

Although companies claim they want to overcome these explicit and implicit biases and hire and promote diverse candidates, they rarely do so in effective ways. When Harvard Business School's emeriti professors David A. Thomas and John Gabarro conducted an in-depth six-year study of leaders in three companies, they found that people of color had to manage their careers more strategically than their white peers did and to prove greater competence before winning promotions.[7] And research by Lynn Perry Wooten, the dean of Cornell University's Dyson School, and Erika Hayes James, the dean of Emory University's Goizueta Business School, shows that Black leaders who do rise to the top are disproportionately handed "glass cliff" assignments, which offer nice rewards but carry a greater risk of failure.[8] Other research, such as Duke University professor Ashleigh

Rosette's studies of Black leaders, has shown widespread racial differences in hiring, performance ratings, promotions, and other outcomes.[9]

There is also an emotional tax associated with being Black in the American workplace. Research by the University of Virginia's Courtney McCluney and Catalyst's Dnika Travis and Jennifer Thorpe-Moscon shows that because Black employees feel a heightened sense of difference among their mostly white peers, their ability to contribute is diminished.[10] "The sense of isolation, of solitude, can take a toll," one leader told them. "It's like facing each day with a core of uncertainty . . . wondering . . . if the floor you're standing on is concrete or dirt . . . solid or not."

Many Black professionals have reported to Toigo that they are expected to be "cultural ambassadors" who address the needs of other Black employees, which leaves them doing two jobs: "the official one the person was hired to do, and a second one as champion for members of the person's minority group," as one put it.[11] Across industries, sectors, and functions, they also experience the "diversity fatigue" that arises from constantly engaging in task forces, trainings, and conversations about race as they are tapped to represent their demographic.

Black leaders in particular struggle with feeling inauthentic at work. Research by McGill University's Patricia Faison Hewlin shows that many minorities feel pressured to create "facades of conformity," suppressing their personal values, views, and attributes to fit in with organizational ones.[12] But as Hewlin and her colleague Anna-Maria Broomes found in a survey of 2,226 workers in various industries and corporate settings, African Americans create these facades more frequently than other minority groups do and feel the inauthenticity more deeply.[13] They might chemically relax (straighten) their hair, conform with coworkers' behavior, "whitewash" their résumés by deleting ethnic-sounding names or companies, hide minority beliefs, and suppress emotions related to workplace racism.

As a result of all the above, Black workers feel less supported, engaged, and committed to their jobs than their non-Black peers do, as research from Georgetown University's Ella Washington, Gallup's Ellyn Maese and Shane McFeely, and others has documented.[14] Black managers report receiving less psychosocial support than their white counterparts do. Black employees are less likely than whites or Hispanics to say that their company's mission or purpose makes them feel their job is important, that their coworkers will do quality work, and that they have opportunities to learn and grow. Black leaders are more likely than white ones to leave their organizations.

It's clear that the norms and cultural defaults of leadership in most organizations create an inhospitable environment that leaves even those Black employees who have advanced feeling like outsiders—and in some cases pushes them out the door.

Relatively high pay and impressive pedigrees don't help much: According to a survey of diverse professionals with bachelor's or graduate degrees and average annual incomes of $100,000 or more that one of us (Laura) conducted with colleagues at the Partnership, a nonprofit organization specializing in diversity and leadership development, African Americans report the lowest levels of both manager and coworker support, commitment, and job fit and the highest levels of feeling inauthentic and wanting to leave their jobs.[15] Studies of Black Harvard Business School and Harvard Law School graduates have similarly found that matriculating from highly respected institutions does not shield one from obstacles.[16] When surveyed years and even decades after graduating, Black Harvard MBAs expressed less satisfaction than their white counterparts with opportunities to do meaningful work, to realize professional accomplishments, and to combine career with personal and family life. "Perhaps it sounds naive, but [coming out of HBS] I did not expect race to have any bearing in my career," one told us. "I was wrong."

## Leading Change

As we said earlier, diversity and inclusion efforts have been gaining traction, and workforces are becoming increasingly multiracial. But given the dearth of Black leaders, we would like to see companies jump-start their efforts in four ways.

### First, move away from the business case and toward a moral one

The dozens of D&I executives we talked to in the course of our research tell us they sometimes feel they've taken the business case for diversity as far as it can go. When Weber Shandwick surveyed 500 chief diversity officers at companies with revenue of $500 million or more, results confirmed that proving that ROI—showing that inclusive teams yield more-creative ideas that appeal to broader customer bases, open new markets, and ultimately drive better performance—is one of the biggest challenges.[17]

The research on this is clear. A 2015 McKinsey report on 366 public companies found that those in the top quartile for ethnic and racial diversity in management were 35% more likely than others to have financial returns above the industry mean.[18] Various studies have shown that teams composed of both white and Black people are more likely to focus on facts, carefully process information, and spur innovation when the organizational culture and leadership support learning across differences.[19]

With the right knowledge, skills, and experience, African American employees and managers can add as much business value as anyone else. They may have greater insights about creating and selling offerings for minority consumer groups that end up appealing to white consumers as well. As one of us (Tony) showed in research with Nitin Nohria, now the dean of Harvard Business School, and Eckerd College's Laura Singleton, some of the most successful Black entrepreneurs are those who—in some cases *because* they were marginalized—built companies to serve their same-race peers, particularly in the personal care, media, and fashion arenas.[20] Examples include the nineteenth-century Black-hair-care trailblazer Madam C. J. Walker, Black Entertainment Television's Robert and Sheila Johnson, and Daymond John, who launched the FUBU clothing line.

So, experts agree that diversity enhances business outcomes when managed well. But given the limited progress African Americans have made in most of corporate America, it seems clear that the sound business arguments for inclusion are not enough. At many companies,

D&I executives still struggle for airtime in the C-suite and for resources that can move their organizations beyond the tokenism of, say, one Black executive in the senior ranks.[21] Their business cases don't appear to have been as persuasive as those presented by their marketing, operations, and accounting colleagues, which have a more direct effect on the bottom line.

And in more progressive companies—ones truly committed to inclusion—a different kind of pushback sometimes occurs: If a team incorporates women, Asians, Latinos, and representatives of the LGBTQ community alongside white men, if it has data geeks and creative types, extroverts and introverts, Harvard MBAs and college dropouts, able-bodied and physically challenged members, isn't it diverse enough? Our answer: Not when teams, especially those at the highest levels, leave out the most marginalized group in the United States.

Thus we turn to the moral case. Many in the U.S. business community have begun to push for a more purpose-driven capitalism that focuses not just on shareholder value but also on shared value—benefits that extend to employees, customers, suppliers, and communities. This movement, toward what the University of Toronto's Sarah Kaplan calls the 360° Corporation, wants corporate leaders to consider both the financial and the ethical implications of all their decisions.[22] We believe that one of its pillars should be proportionate representation and wages for Black Americans.

Why this group in particular? As the *New York Times'* excellent 1619 Project highlighted, we are exactly four centuries away from the start of slavery—the kidnapping, forced labor, mistreatment, and often murder of African people—in the United States. And we are just 154 years away from its end. Although discrimination based on race and other factors was outlawed by the Civil Rights Act of 1964, the effects of slavery and the decades of discrimination and disenfranchisement that followed it continue to hold back many descendants of enslaved people (and those from different circumstances who have the same skin color). Alarmingly, racism and racist incidents are on the rise: According to the FBI, the number of hate crimes committed in the United States rose by 17% from 2016 to 2017, marking the third consecutive year of increases.[23]

We also can't forget that a compelling business case can be—and has been—made for all the atrocities listed above. Indeed, when invoked absent humanistic and ethical principles, a "business case" has legitimated exploitative actions throughout history. White landowners argued that the economic welfare of the colonies and the health of a young country depended on keeping Black people in chains. White business owners in the Jim Crow

South and segregated neighborhoods across the country claimed that sales would suffer if Black customers and residents—who in the absence of land and good jobs had amassed little wealth—were allowed in, because that would turn rich white customers away. And white executives have long benefited because people of color with less access to high-quality education and high-wage employment were forced into low-paying commercial and household jobs, from coal mining and call center work to cleaning, cooking, and caregiving.

So the case for racial diversity and the advancement of African Americans can't be solely about increasing innovation or providing access to and legitimacy in minority markets to maximize revenue and profits. We can't simply ask, "What's the most lucrative thing to do?" We must also ask, "What's the right thing to do?" The imperative should be creating a context in which people of all colors, but especially those who have historically been oppressed, can realize their full potential. This will involve exploring and understanding the racist history that has shaped various groups' access to resources and opportunities and that undergirds contemporary bias. It means emphasizing equity and justice.

How might this work? Starbucks has made some attempts. In the wake of protests following the 2014 fatal shooting of Michael Brown by police in Ferguson,

Missouri, the coffee chain announced RaceTogether, which aimed to spark a national conversation about race relations by having baristas write that phrase on customers' cups. The campaign fell flat because it was perceived more as a profit-minded marketing stunt than as a good-faith effort to change the status quo. Subsequent initiatives, perhaps designed with ethics more squarely in mind, have garnered a more positive response. In 2015 Starbucks launched a hiring program to recruit disadvantaged youths, including African Americans; in 2017 it expanded that program and added one to recruit refugees; and after a racially charged incident at one of its cafés in 2018, it closed all its U.S. cafés for a day of employee antibias training. Consider, too, Nike's decision to launch a marketing campaign headlined by Colin Kaepernick, the NFL quarterback who failed to get picked up by a team after he began kneeling during the national anthem to protest the unfair treatment of African Americans. The campaign created a backlash among anti-Kaepernick consumers and a #BoycottNike hashtag, but the sports apparel brand stood by its tagline: "Believe in something. Even if it means sacrificing everything." We applaud these steps and hope organizations will go even further in learning how to practice racial inclusion in their workplaces.

Some organizations have invoked the moral case for action in other contexts. Think of how Patagonia supports environmental protections by committing to donate either 1% of sales or 10% of profits (whichever is larger) to advocacy groups. And recall that Dick's Sporting Goods pulled assault weapons and high-capacity magazines from its stores following the Parkland, Florida, school shooting, even though it projected—accurately—that the move would mean a $250 million hit to sales. (It's important to note that over the long term, none of those companies suffered from their choices.)

Such stances take courage. But by combining the business case and the moral one, leaders can make a more powerful argument for supporting Black advancement.

## Second, encourage open conversations about race

As Dartmouth College's Ella Bell and the University of Pretoria's Stella Nkomo note in the introduction to our book, "organizations are *in* society, not apart from it." And although President Obama's election brought some talk of a postracial era in the United States, the stories and statistics that have come out in the past few years show that racism still exists, which means that race still

matters and needs to be discussed, candidly and frequently, in the workplace.

Those conversations will not immediately feel comfortable. Research shows that although many people are
happy to talk about "diversity" or "inclusion," their en-
thusiasm drops significantly when the subject is "race."[24]
Most of us don't like to think very hard about where minorities sit and what power they wield (or don't) within
our organizations—much less discuss it. When we examine who has been excluded in what ways over what
period of time, the concept of white privilege might come
up. And majority-group employees might express concerns about reverse discrimination. (According to an
Ernst & Young study of 1,000 U.S. workers, one-third of
respondents said that a corporate focus on diversity has
overlooked white men.[25]) Charged topics like these can
provoke resentment, anger, and shame. But we need real
exchanges about them if we want to dispel the notion that
corporations are pure meritocracies and to ensure that
everyone feels heard, supported, and authentic at work.

Senior leaders—most of whom are white men—must
set the tone. Why? In one survey, nearly 40% of Black
employees said they feel it is *never* acceptable to speak
out about experiences of bias—a silence that can become
corrosive.[26] Another study showed that among Black
professionals who aspire to senior leadership positions,

the most frequently adopted strategy is to avoid talking about race or other issues of inequality, for fear of being labeled an agitator. Other research has indicated that the only CEOs and lower-level managers not penalized for championing diversity are white men.[27]

To create a culture of psychological safety and pave the way for open communication will require a top-down directive and modeling through informal and formal discussions in which people are asked to share ideas, ask questions, and address issues without fear of reprisal. Managers down the line will need training in encouraging and guiding such exchanges, including inviting Black employees and leaders to share their experiences—the good, the bad, and the ugly. Participants should be trained to prepare for such conversations by reflecting on their own identities and the comments and situations that trigger strong emotions in them. As detailed by Columbia University's Valerie Purdie Greenaway and the University of Virginia's Martin Davidson, the goal is to shift the entire organization to a racial-learning orientation.[28]

Again, a movement from another context—#MeToo—sheds light on how to do so. Revelations of abuse and harassment and the outpouring of women's stories that followed, many about incidents that happened in the workplace, forced corporate leaders to focus on those issues. Bad actors were fired, women felt empowered to speak up, and awareness of gender discrimination increased. Although #BlackLivesMatter has had similar success highlighting and sparking discussions around police brutality, there is no #BlackLivesAtWork. There should be.

We see some positive signs on this front. Over the past few years several prominent leaders, including PwC's Tim Ryan, Interpublic Group's Michael Roth, Kaiser Permanente's Bernard Tyson, and AT&T's Randall Stephenson, have initiated companywide discussions of race. For example, PwC brought in Mellody Hobson, president and co-CEO of Ariel Investments and a prominent African American leader, to talk to employees about being "color-brave" instead of "color-blind" at work, and it has offered guides for continuing the discussion. At Morgan Stanley, global head of D&I Susan Reid has promoted intimate conversations about race in networking groups and an hour-long forum on race in the current social climate. The latter was moderated by the company's vice chairman and featured its chief marketing officer, its head of prime brokerage, and a *Fortune* reporter who covers racial issues; it was attended by 1,500 employees, and videos of the event were shared across the firm. Greenaway and Davidson also point to a mostly white male financial services firm that instituted Know Us, a program of small-group cross-race dialogues on racially relevant topics.[29]

Over time these conversations will start to happen informally and organically in groups and among individuals at all levels of an organization, deepening interpersonal cross-race relationships. In one consulting company cited by Greenaway and Davidson, non-Black employees started a book club open to all but focused on Black writers; the group has visited African American museums and historical sites.[30] One-on-one interactions can be even more meaningful, as the psychologist colleagues Karen Samuels (who is white) and Kathryn Fraser (who is Black) describe: "It was important to name our racial and cultural differences and to examine how my perspective was naive regarding her reality," Samuels explains.[31]

## Third, revamp D&I programs

Any corporate diversity and inclusion program is better than none, but most that exist today are not designed to sustain a focus on racial equity. Many are siloed within the HR department, lack C-suite support, or are given to women or people of color to manage in addition to their day jobs. Some are more show than go, resting on philosophical statements about inclusion rather than outlining concrete steps for advancing nonwhites. Others limit their efforts to antibias and cultural competence training—preempting problems but, again, not propelling anyone forward. Most take a broad-brush approach to diversity, attempting to serve all minorities plus white women, LGBTQ employees, and those who are neurodiverse or disabled and offering uniform training and leadership development that ignore historical patterns of exclusion, marginality, and disadvantage for each group. They might focus too heavily on recruitment and retention—filling the pipeline and high-potential groups with Black employees but failing to support them past middle-management roles. Most troubling, as Courtney McCluney and San Francisco State University's Verónica Rabelo have shown, a significant portion of D&I programs try to "manage Blackness"—that is, impose "desirable" and "professional" (read: white) norms and expectations on rising African American stars, thus preserving rather than shifting the status quo.[32] They train Black executives to fit into the existing organizational culture rather than encourage them to broaden it by bringing their true and most productive selves to work.

How can we improve such programs? By tackling their shortcomings one by one. Here are several steps organizations can take.

- Give D&I sustained C-suite support and recognize and reward the people who contribute to its initiatives—for example, by having your chief diversity officer report directly to the CEO and tracking inclusion initiative participation in performance reviews and promotion and pay raise discussions.

- Equip and invite white men to take up the mantle—say, by bringing them into D&I programs and assigning some of them to leadership roles.

- Challenge those running D&I efforts to set clear goals for how representation, organizational networks, and access to resources should change across functions and levels over time and how Black employees' perceptions, engagement, and well-being should improve, and then measure the efforts' effectiveness with data analysis and qualitative surveys.

- Shift from preventative measures, such as anti-bias training, to proactive ones, such as upping the number of Black candidates considered for open positions and stretch roles.

- Abandon one-size-fits-all and color-blind leadership-development practices in favor of courses and coaching tailored to specific groups— or better yet, adopt personalized plans that recognize the multifaceted nature of each individual.

- Help Black employees and rising leaders throughout their careers, including teaching managers the skills they need to support D&I efforts.

- Stop asking Black employees to blend in; instead, emphasize the value of a workplace that embraces all styles and behaviors.

In sum, D&I needs to be an ethos that permeates the entire organization, championed not just by the HR department but by everyone, and especially managers, so that its importance is clear. The Toigo Foundation's leaders draw a parallel between this idea and the total quality management movement of the 1980s, which, with top-down support and the establishment of key performance indicators, became a pervasive way of working and thinking that filtered down to every function and level.

Few companies to date have taken diversity and inclusion that far. But some are moving in the right direction, including JPMorgan Chase, which in 2016 launched a board- and CEO-supported Advancing Black Leaders strategy—staffed and managed separately from other D&I initiatives—focused on filling the firm's pipeline with Black talent and retaining and promoting those workers. SAP's Black Employee Network helped launch its partnership with Delaware State University through Project Propel, which offers tech training and skills development to students from historically Black colleges and universities (HBCUs), with the goal of building an employee pipeline. The network also encouraged SAP to sponsor Silicon Valley's Culture Shifting Weekend, which brings together more than 200 African American and Hispanic executives, entrepreneurs, innovators, and social impact leaders to discuss diversifying the tech industry. Pfizer tracks numerous D&I metrics and notes that 21% of its workforce—21,000 people—are actively involved in its D&I efforts.

## Finally, manage career development across all life stages

African Americans today are securing good university educations in record numbers. HBCUs, in particular, create a sizable pipeline of young talent for organizations to tap into. Companies can, of course, step up their campus recruiting efforts, but efforts to advance Black leaders must extend far beyond that.

If more African Americans are to rise through the ranks, robust—and careful—investment in retention and development is required. Research by the University of Georgia's Kecia Thomas and colleagues has shown that many Black women get this kind of support early in their careers, but it comes with a price: They are treated like "pets" whom white leaders are happy to groom, but the further they progress, the more that favored status begins to undermine them.[33] Those who reject the pet identity, meanwhile, are perceived as threatening and face hostility and distancing from coworkers.

Mentoring is useful, and our study of Black HBS graduates shows that they were more likely than their white peers to have been formally assigned to mentors.[34] But they derived less value from the relationship and said that informal mentorship—having senior executives (white or minority) connect with them naturally through work groups or common interests—was more effective. "A mentor helps you navigate the power structure of the firm, especially when there is no one in senior management who looks like you," one study participant told us.

Early in their careers, Black employees need safe spaces to grow and develop and to experience authentic failures and successes without being subsumed in narratives of racial limitation. Managers and mentors can provide the necessary cover. We found that the Black Harvard MBAs who did reach top management positions (13% of women, 19% of men) had been bolstered by networks of supporters.

Sponsorship—that is, recommending Black employees for promotions and stretch assignments—is even more important. Other key factors that have propelled Black Harvard MBAs into senior executive roles are line or general management experience and global assignments. With many qualified and ambitious people vying for such opportunities, politics often plays a role. So African Americans need more influential people in their corners, pressing their cases to decision makers.

Candid feedback early on is also critical. This doesn't mean pushing protégés to assimilate (to look and act "more white"); as we've shown, that's counterproductive. It should focus on identifying and enhancing their unique strengths, overcoming skill or knowledge weaknesses, and positioning them to realize their full potential.

At later stages of their careers, Black executives should be seriously considered for high-stakes and high-profile positions and supported in the pursuit of outside interests, such as board seats, that enhance visibility. And while taking care not to tokenize but rather to create opportunities for multiple candidates, organizations can highlight those executives as role models who redefine norms of leadership and can encourage them to pass that baton by transferring connections and endorsements, sharing wisdom through storytelling, and creating opportunities for the next generation to assume senior roles. Needs differ by career stage, a fact that most published models of diversity and inclusion do not address but that is embedded in impactful programs such as the Toigo Foundation, the Partnership, and the Executive Leadership Council.

. . .

Despite antidiscrimination laws and increasing corporate investment in diversity efforts, race continues to be a major barrier to advancement in the U.S. workplace. We are far from realizing the principles of equal opportunity and meritocracy. Rather than looking to the few Black leaders who have succeeded as exemplars of exceptionalism who have beaten almost insurmountable odds, we must learn from their insights and experiences along with the experiences of those who didn't make it to the top. Perhaps more important, we need to understand why existing inclusion initiatives have made so little difference. If organizations really want a representative workforce that includes more than one or two Black leaders, their approach must change.

Our hope is that once companies understand the reality of the Black experience, they will embrace and champion policies and programs that actually help to level the playing field—and that where there aren't yet best practices, they will begin the conversations and experiments that will lead to them. This will be hard and often uncomfortable work. But we believe it's worth it, not only for African Americans but also for the many other under-represented or marginalized groups. Now more than ever before, organizations and society should strive to benefit from the experiences, knowledge, and skills of all, not just a few. And while government policies can help, we believe that corporate leaders can have a much more powerful and immediate impact. As then-Senator Obama said in 2008, *"Change will not come if we wait for some other person or if we wait for some other time. We are the ones we've been waiting for. We are the change that we seek."*

**TAKEAWAYS**

At most large U.S. and multinational organizations, diversity and inclusion have become imperatives, but the power of African Americans in these organizations remains limited and their experiences leave them feeling like outsiders. To maximize the human potential of everyone in the workplace, organizations should take these specific steps toward racial justice:

✓ Shift the conversation from an exclusive focus on the most lucrative thing to do to the right thing to do with regard to race.

✓ Encourage open dialogue about race.

✓ Revamp diversity and inclusion programs to clarify goals and focus on proactive steps.

✓ Manage career development across all life stages,
from campus recruitment to the consideration of
Black executives for top jobs.

## NOTES

1. "Korn Ferry Study Reveals United States Black P&L Leaders Are
Some of the Highest Performing Executives in the U.S. C-Suite,"
kornferry.com, October 8, 2019, https://www.kornferry.com/about
-us//press/korn-ferry-study-reveals-united-states-black-pl-leaders
-are-some-of-the-highest-performing-executives-in-the-us-c-suite;
and Muriel E. Shockley and Elizabeth L. Holloway, "African
American Women as Change Agents in the White Academy,"
in *Race, Work, and Leadership: New Perspectives on the Black
Experience*, ed. Laura Morgan Roberts, Anthony J. Mayo, and
David A. Thomas (Boston: Harvard Business Review Press, 2019),
253–273.

2. Katherine W. Phillips, "How Diversity Makes Us Smarter:
Being Around People Who Are Different from Us Makes Us More
Creative, More Diligent and Harder-Working," *Scientific American*, October 1, 2014, https://www.scientificamerican.com/article
/how-diversity-makes-us-smarter/.

3. "More Than 4.5 Million African Americans Now Hold a
Four-Year College Degree," *Journal of Blacks in Higher Education*
(2009): http://www.jbhe.com/news_views/64_degrees.html.

Toward a Racially Just Workplace

4. Jamiles Lartey, "Median Wealth of Black Americans 'Will Fall to Zero by 2053,' Warns New Report," *Guardian* (US edition), September 13, 2017, https://www.theguardian.com/inequality/2017/sep/13/median-wealth-of-black-7americans-will-fall-to-zero-by-2053-warns-new-report.

5. Stacy Jones, "White Men Account for 72% of Corporate Leadership at 16 of the *Fortune* 500 Companies," *Fortune*, June 9, 2017, https://fortune.com/2017/06/09/white-men-senior-executives-fortune-500-companies-diversity-data/.

6. Anthony J. Mayo and Laura Morgan Roberts, "Pathways to Leadership" in Roberts, Mayo, and Thomas, eds., *Race, Work, and Leadership*, 41–72.

7. David A. Thomas and John J. Gabarro, *Breaking Through: The Making of Minority Executives in Corporate America* (Boston: Harvard Business School Publishing, 1999).

8. Lynn Perry Wooten and Erika Hayes James, "The Glass Cliff," in Roberts, Mayo, and Thomas, eds., *Race, Work, and Leadership*, 323–339.

9. Andrew M. Carton and Ashleigh Shelby Rosette, "Explaining Bias against Black Leaders: Integrating Theory on Information Processing and Goal-Based Stereotyping," *Academy of Management Journal* 54, no. 6 (April 2012): https://journals.aom.org/doi/10.5465/amj.2009.0745; and "Black Quarterbacks Take Hits in the Media as Well as on the Field," *Fuqua Insights*, January 3, 2012, https://www.fuqua.duke.edu/duke-fuqua-insights/black-quarterback-take-hits-media.

10. Dnika J. Travis, Jennifer Thorpe-Moscon, and Courtney McCluney, "Report: Emotional Tax: How Black Women and Men Pay More at Work and How Leaders Can Take Action," *Catalyst*, October 11, 2016, https://www.catalyst.org/research/emotional-tax-how-black-women-and-men-pay-more-at-work-and-how-leaders-can-take-action/.

11.  Toigo Foundation (Nancy Sims, Sue Toigo, Maura Allen, and Toni Cornelius), "From C-Suite to Startups" in Roberts, Mayo, and Thomas, eds., *Race, Work, and Leadership*, 209–222.

12.  Patricia Faison Hewlin, "Wearing the Cloak: Antecedents and Consequences of Creating Facades of Conformity," *Journal of Applied Psychology* 94, no. 3 (May 2009): https://pubmed.ncbi.nlm .nih.gov/19450009/.

13.  Patricia Faison Hewlin and Anna-Maria Broomes, "Authenticity in the Workplace" in Roberts, Mayo, and Thomas, eds., *Race, Work, and Leadership*, 135–149.

14.  Ella F. Washington, Ellyn Maese, and Shane McFeely, "Workplace Engagement and the Glass Ceiling" in Roberts, Mayo, and Thomas, eds., *Race, Work, and Leadership*, 115–134.

15.  Stacy Blake-Beard, Laura Morgan Roberts, Beverly Edgehill, and Ella F. Washington, "Feeling Connected" in Roberts, Mayo, and Thomas, eds., *Race, Work, and Leadership*, 151–169.

16.  Mayo and Roberts, "Pathways to Leadership"; and David B. Wilkins and Bryon Fong, "Intersectionality and the Careers of Black Women Lawyers" in Roberts, Mayo, and Thomas, eds., *Race, Work, and Leadership*, 73–111.

17.  Weber Shandwick, *Chief Diversity Officers Today: Paving the Way for Diversity & Inclusion Success*, https://www.webershandwick .com/wp-content/uploads/2019/09/Chief-Diversity-Officers-Today -report.pdf.

18.  Vivian Hunt, Dennis Layton, and Sara Prince, "Why Diversity Matters," McKinsey & Company (website), January 1, 2015, https:// www.mckinsey.com/business-functions/organization/our-insights /why-diversity-matters.

19. Phillips, "How Diversity Makes Us Smarter."

20. Mayo and Roberts, "Pathways to Leadership."

21. Jeff Green, "Most Diversity Executives Say They Lack Power to Push Change," Bloomberg, March 1, 2019, https://www.bloomberg.com/news/articles/2019-03-01/most-diversity-executives-say-they-lack-power-to-push-change; and Frank Dobbin and Alexandra Kalev, "Why Diversity Programs Fail," *Harvard Business Review*, July–August 2016, https://hbr.org/2016/07/why-diversity-programs-fail.

22. Sarah Kaplan, *The 360° Corporation: From Stakeholder Trade-offs to Transformation* (Palo Alto: Stanford University Press, 2019), https://sarahkaplan.info/the360corporation/.

23. John Eligon, "Hate Crimes Increase for the Third Consecutive Year, F.B.I. Reports," *New York Times*, November 13, 2018, https://www.nytimes.com/2018/11/13/us/hate-crimes-fbi-2017.html.

24. Douglas Hartmann, "Happy Talk About Diversity Avoids Difficult Racial Issues," Scholars Strategy Network (website), March 1, 2012, https://scholars.org/brief/happy-talk-about-diversity-avoids-difficult-racial-issues; Joyce M. Bell and Douglas Hartmann, "Diversity in Everyday Discourse: The Cultural Ambiguities and Consequences of 'Happy Talk,'" *American Sociological Review* 72 (December 2007): https://journals.sagepub.com/doi/pdf/10.1177/000312240707200603.

25. Ruth Umoh, "A Recent Study Says Some White Men Feel Excluded at Work," Make It, cnbc.com, October 12, 2017, https://www.cnbc.com/2017/10/12/a-recent-study-says-some-white-men-feel-excluded-at-work.html.

26. Sylvia Ann Hewlett, Melinda Marshall, and Trudy Bourgeois, "People Suffer at Work When They Can't Discuss the Racial Bias They Face Outside of It," hbr.org, July 10, 2017, https://hbr.org/2017

/07/people-suffer-at-work-when-they-cant-discuss-the-racial-bias
-they-face-outside-of-it.

27. Stefanie K. Johnson and David R. Hekman, "Women and
Minorities Are Penalized for Promoting Diversity," hbr.org,
March 23, 2016, https://hbr.org/2016/03/women-and-minorities
-are-penalized-for-promoting-diversity.

28. Valerie Purdie Greenaway and Martin N. Davidson, "How to
Design for Real Inclusion," SHRM, September 26, 2019, https://
blog.hrps.org/blogpost/How-to-Design-for-Real-Inclusion.

29. Greenaway and Davidson, "How to Design for Real Inclusion."

30. Valeria Purdie Greenaway and Martin N. Davidson, "Is D&I
About Us?" in Roberts, Mayo, and Thomas, eds., *Race, Work, and
Leadership*, 311–322.

31. Kathryn Fraser and Karen Samuels, "A Million Gray Areas"
in Roberts, Mayo, and Thomas, eds., *Race, Work, and Leadership*,
239–252.

32. Courtney L. McCluney and Verónica Caridad Rabelo, "Managing Diversity, Managing Blackness?" in Roberts, Mayo, and
Thomas, eds., *Race, Work, and Leadership*, 373–387.

33. K. M. Thomas, J. Johnson-Bailey, R. E. Phelps, N. M. Tran, and
L. Johnson, "Moving from Pet to Threat: Narratives of Professional
Black Women," in *The Psychological Health of Women of Color: In-
tersections, Challenges, and Opportunities*, ed. L. Comas-Diaz and
B. Green (Westport, CT: Praeger, 2013).

34. Mayo and Roberts, "Pathways to Leadership."

*Adapted from "Toward a Racially Just Workplace," on hbr.org, November 11, 2019
(product #BG1906).*

# UPDATE YOUR DE&I PLAYBOOK

by Joan C. Williams and James D. White

**W**hite Americans are finally starting to understand that racism is structural. The problem is not just a matter of a few bad apples, and it certainly won't be solved by a few good conversations. To dismantle structural racism in our organizations, we must change our cultures.

"But how?" companies wonder. They have a chief diversity office. They've done bias trainings. They have employee resource groups (ERGs). They celebrate Black History Month. Why are their efforts not working?

Chief diversity officers (CDOs), bias training, and ERGs do not address subtle and persistent forms of bias. Four decades of studies show that white men have to prove themselves less than any other demographic group; their successes are noticed more and their mistakes noticed less.[1] How does this play out? Here's one example: At the request of a company woke enough to care, one of us (Williams) did an audit of performance evaluations and found that mistakes were mentioned in 43% of the reviews of employees of color but in only 26% of the reviews of white men. And that's just the beginning. Three decades of studies show that white men are also more likely than others to get away with personality quirks and interpersonal issues.[2] Take anger: 56.1% of white male lawyers feel free to express anger when it's justified, but only 39.6% of women lawyers of color do.[3] Being seen as an "angry Black man"—or an angry woman of any race—typically is not a good career move. No wonder the percentage of CEOs who are white men has fallen only 4% in over a decade, from 93.4% in 2005 to 89.4% in 2017.[4] And nearly 70% of senior leadership (VP, senior VP, and C-suite) positions are held by white men, suggesting that little will change at the top.[5]

For all the time and treasure spent on diversity, equity, and inclusion (DE&I) by U.S. companies, the failure to deal with structural racism has predictable results.

Google reportedly spent $114 million on DE&I in 2014, but this year reported that African Americans make up only 3.7% of its workforce, and 2.6% of leadership roles.[6]

One of us (James D. White) is an African American former CEO who led a turnaround at Jamba Juice that wove diversity into the fabric of his company. In his seven years at Jamba Juice, he tripled the diversity of the top three levels and increased the diversity of the top two levels from 20% to 50%. Over that same period the company's market cap soared 500%—performance that we argue resulted from James's efforts to create a true meritocracy that holds every group to the same standards. When the whole workforce can bring its talents to the table, results are better than when only some people can.

White's coauthor, Joan C. Williams, is a white researcher who has documented how subtle forms of racial and gender bias are transmitted through companies' culture and systems, and how evidence-based "bias interrupters" can change those systems and routines. In one experiment at the University of Kansas, social psychologist Monica Biernat gave subjects Williams's open-sourced two-and-a-half-page "Identifying and Interrupting Bias in Performance Evaluations" worksheet.[7] Just doing that—nothing more—sharply increased the bonuses of Black men and women and white women. Bias interrupters use the very same tools companies use to solve any problem they care about: evidence, metrics, and goals. Their absence in the DE&I context speaks volumes.

Addressing structural racism requires changing the structures that reinforce racism. In this article, we meld White's approach with Williams's to propose a new four-component DE&I model to do just that.

## 1. Make Sure the DE&I Leader Has the Authority to Make Systemic Change.

For years, the standard DE&I playbook has been to hire a CDO with a budget for consultants and enrichment programs. But you can't build capacity if the problem is not with the diverse talent but with the culture that determines their future. And hiring a consultant to give bias training is fine, but doing anything *once* cannot change a corporate culture that reinforces itself day after day.

Sweeping overhauls require support from the top that only a CEO can deliver. When White became CEO of Jamba Juice, he went structural in ways most CDOs could never accomplish. When he was hired, all 10 members of the board of directors were white men. White championed two new board members, both women, one African American. White firmly believes that the board's new range of voices changed the way the company thought about its people and its business. Though White would have led the same way with a less diverse board, he might not have been *supported* in the same way—which may well have limited his ability to undertake the broad structural changes he accomplished.

DE&I initiatives either need to be led by the CEO, or companies need to empower their CDO with substantial authority. Better yet—the CEO may also serve as CDO; Nielsen's David Kenny is one example of this approach. The CDO has to have the power to make the kinds of systemic changes we describe below.

## 2. Change the Way Glamour Work Is Assigned.

Glamour work positions employees for promotions. Crucially, middle-level managers are typically the people who control who gets these high-profile assignments; that's why white men so often get channeled to the top despite the best efforts of the CDO. When White took over at Jamba Juice, management was 80% white men; by the end of his first year, half of the managers were women and people of color. He pulled off that feat by changing the way career-enhancing work was assigned.

His approach was to appoint action learning teams (ALTs) to accomplish key business goals, including opening new distribution channels in airports and moving into global markets. ALTs are cross-functional teams of 15 to 20 people, with breakout groups of between five and eight people who are laser-focused on solving well-defined problems. ALTs were given release time from their regular jobs and a 90-day deadline. The theory behind action learning is that the people on the ground know best what's working well and how to fix what's not. You just need to choose the right talent with the right mix of skills to solve a specific, well-defined business challenge. White purposely chose previously overlooked employees for this glamour work, which meant that the teams were far more diverse than the company's workforce as a whole. By reconceiving the mechanism for assigning glamour work, White created a pipeline that increased diversity at the top.

## 3. Change the Incentives and Enhance the Capacity of Middle Management.

At every organization White has helped lead, he's found that middle managers are the key to changing the culture. Effective policies *enable* inclusion, but middle-level managers hold the key to delivering it.

At Jamba Juice, he instituted a new incentive system. In this new system, up to 20% of store managers' compensation was determined by engagement, climate, and organizational health scores. White used a variant of the Gallup $Q^{12}$ survey; another useful tool is Williams's Workplace Experience Survey, a 10-minute survey that pinpoints every basic pattern of racial and gender bias, where it is playing out, and its impact on outcome measures like belonging and intent to stay.

Addressing structural racism requires managers who understand the specific ways bias commonly privileges one group, so they can understand the reasoning behind the new policies, procedures, and incentives. Accomplishing this will require bias training that does more than just explore the cognitive bases of bias without providing concrete strategies for interrupting it. Williams's Individual Bias Interrupters workshop does this by explaining how bias plays out on the ground and giving managers time to brainstorm ways they personally would feel comfortable interrupting it. But that's just one example: Facebook's inclusion trainings also give people a chance to brainstorm ways to interrupt bias. Facebook also deeply integrates bias awareness into multiple trainings. Again, go structural: What's needed is not just one training; all of a company's trainings—from on-boarding to leadership programming—should seamlessly build in continuing education on how bias enters into company culture, at many evidence-based, meet-you-where-you're-at touch points.

# 4. Debias HR Systems.

Williams's research documents in detail how business systems transmit both racial and gender bias. In a national survey of lawyers, her team found that people of color and white women reported they lacked a fair shot at getting hired, receiving fair performance evaluations, getting mentorship and networking opportunities, receiving high-quality assignments, and getting paid and promoted fairly—all at much higher levels than white men.[8] In industry after industry, Williams's team has documented that other groups' experience diverges from white men's. Women of color experience the largest difference, with men of color and white women typically in between. The differences are often dramatic. Only a third of white male engineers reported they had to prove themselves more than their colleagues did, compared to two-thirds of women and people of color.[9] Women lawyers of color report that they get equal access to high-quality assignments at a level 28 percentage points lower than white men.[10] In another study, only about a quarter of white male architects reported bias in compensation; two-thirds of Black women did.

Debiasing HR systems starts by appointing an ALT that includes the CEO or another executive sponsor, the CDO, the head of HR, some outstanding and receptive managers, a data analyst and others who receive release time, a mandate, and a deadline to debias existing HR systems. The most straightforward approach is to adapt Williams's open-sourced toolkits, which use evidence to identify key metrics and establish baselines to measure progress—again, the tools we use to address any challenge we are truly committed to solving. Going structural yields real results: When one insurance company developed objective criteria and rated all applicants using the same rubric, it ended up offering jobs to 46% more minority candidates (see chapter 7, "How the Best Bosses Interrupt Bias on Their Teams").

. . .

In most organizations, CDOs don't control any of the relevant HR systems, much less all of them, and eliminating bias in just one system means that bias will remain everywhere else, silently but effectively powering the invisible escalator for white men while leaving everyone else stuck toiling up the stairs. To address structural racism effectively, the CDO—whether that's the CEO or not—needs the authority to change both formal and informal systems, instituting changes that typically will help both people of color of both sexes and women of all races.

**TAKEAWAYS**

Chief diversity officers, bias training, and employee resource groups have not succeeded in dismantling structural racism because they don't address subtle and persistent forms of bias. Instead, companies must take action to confront and change the structures that reinforce racism. A four-component DE&I model can help:

✓ Make sure the DE&I leader has the authority to make systemic change. Sweeping overhauls require support from the top that only a CEO can deliver.

✓ Change the way glamour work is assigned. Glamour work positions employees for promotions; by reconceiving the mechanism for assigning it, it's possible to create a pipeline to increase diversity at the top.

✓ **Change the incentives and enhance the capacity of middle management.** Effective policies *enable* inclusion, but middle-level managers hold the key to *delivering* it.

✓ **Debias HR systems.** Success requires a high-level team, a mandate, and a deadline.

## NOTES

1. Master Bibliography, biasinterrupters.org, https://biasinterrupters
.org/wp-content/uploads/Bias-Interrupters-Master-Bibliography
.pdf.

2. Master Bibliography, biasinterrupters.org.

3. Joan C. Williams, Marina Multhaup, Su Li, and Rachel Korn, "You Can't Change What You Can't See: Interrupting Racial & Gender Bias in the Legal Profession," Minority Corporate Counsel Association, https://www.mcca.com/wp-content/uploads/2018/09 /You-Cant-Change-What-You-Cant-See-Executive-Summary.pdf.

4. Richard L. Zweigenhaft, "The Highest Paid CEOs: Still White, Still Male," Society Pages, August 1, 2019, https://thesocietypages .org/specials/the-highest-paid-ceos-still-white-still-male/.

5. Alexis Krivkovich, Marie-Claude Nadeau, Kelsey Robinson, Nicole Robinson, Irina Starikova, and Lareina Yee, "Women in the Workplace 2018," McKinsey & Company, October 23, 2018, https://www.mckinsey.com/featured-insights/gender-equality /women-in-the-workplace-2018.

6. Pamela Newkirk, "Diversity Has Become a Booming Business. So Where Are the Results?" *Time*, October 10, 2019, https://time.com/5696943/diversity-business/; Google Diversity

Annual Report 2020, accessed August 26, 2020, https://kstatic
.googleusercontent.com/files/25badfc6b6d1b33f3b87372ff7545d79
261520d821e6ee9a82c4ab2de42a01216be2156bc5a60ae3337ffe7176
d90b8b2b3000891ac6e516a650ecebf0e3f866.

7. Center for WorkLife Law, "Bias Interrupters for Performance
Evaluations," biasinterrupters.org, accessed August 26, 2020,
https://biasinterrupters.org/wp-content/uploads/Identifying-Bias
-in-Performance-Evaluations-Guide-no-citations.pdf.

8. American Bar Association, *Bias Interrupters*, accessed
August 26, 2020, https://www.americanbar.org/groups/diversity
/women/initiatives_awards/bias-interrupters/.

9. Joan C. Williams, Su Li, Roberta Rincon, and Peter Finn, "Climate Control: Gender and Racial Bias in Engineering?" Society of
Women Engineers, accessed August 26, 2020, https://research.swe
.org/climate-control/.

10. American Bar Association, *Bias Interrupters*.

*Adapted from "Update Your DE&I Playbook," on hbr.org, July 15, 2020 (product
H05QK6).*

# 5

# "NUMBERS TAKE US ONLY SO FAR"

by Maxine Williams

I was once evicted from an apartment because I was Black. I had secured a lovely place on the banks of Lake Geneva through an agent and therefore hadn't met the owner in person before signing the lease. Once my family and I moved in and the color of my skin was clear to see, the landlady asked us to leave. If she had known that I was Black, I was told, she would never have rented to me.

Terrible as it felt at the time, her directness was useful to me. It meant I didn't have to scour the facts looking for some other, nonracist rationale for her sudden rejection.

Many people have been denied housing, bank loans, jobs, promotions, and more because of their race. But they're rarely told that's the reason, as I was—particularly in the workplace. For one thing, such discrimination is illegal. For another, executives tend to think—and have a strong desire to believe—that they're hiring and promoting people fairly when they aren't. (Research shows that individuals who view themselves as objective are often the ones who apply the most unconscious bias.) Though managers don't cite or (usually) even perceive race as a factor in their decisions, they use ambiguous assessment criteria to filter out people who aren't like them, research by Kellogg professor Lauren Rivera shows. People in marginalized racial and ethnic groups are deemed more often than whites to be "not the right cultural fit" or "not ready" for high-level roles; they're taken out of the running because their "communication style" is somehow off the mark. They're left only with lingering suspicions that their identity is the real issue, especially when decision makers' bias is masked by good intentions.

I work in the field of diversity. I've also been Black my whole life. So I know that underrepresented people in the workplace yearn for two things: The first is to hear that they're not crazy to suspect, at times, that there's a connection between negative treatment and bias. The second is to be offered institutional support.

The first need has a clear path to fulfillment. When we encounter colleagues or friends who have been mistreated and who believe that their identity may be the reason, we should acknowledge that it's fair to be suspicious. There's no leap of faith here—numerous studies show how pervasive such bias still is.

But how can we address the second need? In an effort to find valid, scalable ways to counteract or reverse bias and promote diversity, organizations are turning to people analytics—a relatively new field in business operations and talent management that replaces gut decisions with data-driven practices. People analytics aspires to be "evidence based." And for some HR issues—such as figuring out how many job interviews are needed to assess a candidate, or determining how employees' work commutes affect their job satisfaction—it is. Statistically significant findings have led to some big changes in organizations. Unfortunately, companies that try to apply analytics to the challenges of underrepresented groups at work often complain that the relevant data sets don't include enough people to produce reliable insights—the sample size, the $n$, is too small. Basically they're saying, "If only there were more of you, we could tell you why there are so few of you."

Companies have access to more data than they realize, however. To supplement a small $n$, they can venture out and look at the larger context in which they operate. But data volume alone won't give leaders the insight they need to increase diversity in their organizations. They must also take a closer look at the individuals from underrepresented groups who work for them—those who barely register on the analytics radar.

## Supplementing the *N*

Nonprofit research organizations are doing important work that sheds light on how bias shapes hiring and advancement in various industries and sectors. For example, a study by the Ascend Foundation showed that in 2013 white men and white women in five major Silicon Valley firms were 154% more likely to become executives than their Asian counterparts. And though both race and gender were factors in the glass ceiling for Asians, race had 3.7 times the impact that gender did.

It took two more years of research and analysis—using data on several hundred thousand employees, drawn from the EEOC's aggregation of all Bay Area technology firms and from the individual reports of 13 U.S. tech companies—before Ascend determined how bias affected the prospects of Blacks and Hispanics. Among those groups it again found that, overall, race had a greater negative impact than gender on advancement from the professional to the executive level. In the Bay Area white women fared worse than white men but much better than all Asians, Hispanics, and Blacks. Minority women faced the biggest obstacle to entering the executive ranks. Black and Hispanic women were severely challenged by both their low numbers at the professional level and their lower chances of rising from professional to executive. Asian women, who had more representation at the professional level than other minorities, had the lowest chances of moving up from professional to executive. An analysis of national data found similar results.

By analyzing industry or sector data on underrepresented groups—and examining patterns in hiring, promotions, and other decisions about talent—we can better manage the problems and risks in our own organizations. Tech companies may look at the Ascend reports and say, "Hey, let's think about what's happening with our competitors' talent. There's a good chance it's happening here, too." Their HR teams might then add a layer of career tracking for women of color, for example, or create training programs for managing diverse teams.

Another approach is to extrapolate lessons from other companies' analyses. We might look, for instance, at Red Ventures, a Charlotte-based digital media company. Red Ventures is diverse by several measures. (It has a Latino

CEO, and about 40% of its employees are people of color.) But that doesn't mean there aren't problems to solve. When I met with its top executives, they told me they had recently done an analysis of performance reviews at the firm and found that internalized stereotypes were having a negative effect on Black and Latino employees' self-assessments. On average, members of those two groups rated their performance 30% lower than their managers did (whereas white male employees scored their performance 10% higher than their managers did). The study also uncovered a correlation between racial isolation and negative self-perception. For example, people of color who worked in engineering generally rated themselves lower than those who worked in sales, where there were more Blacks and Latinos. These patterns were consistent at all levels, from junior to senior staff.

In response, the HR team at Red Ventures trained employees in how to do self-assessments, and that has started to close the gap for Blacks and Latinos (who more recently rated themselves 22% lower than their managers did). Hallie Cornetta, the company's VP of human capital, explained that the training "focused on the importance of completing quantitative and qualitative self-assessments honestly, in a way that shows how employees personally view their performance across our five key dimensions, rather than how they assume their manager or peers view their performance." She added: "We then shared tangible examples of what 'exceptional' versus 'solid' versus 'needs improvement' looks like in these dimensions to remove some of the subjectivity and help minority—and all—employees assess with greater direction and confidence."

## Getting Personal

Once we've gone broader by supplementing the *n*, we can go deeper by examining individual cases. This is critical. Algorithms and statistics do not capture what it feels like to be the only Black or Hispanic team member or the effect that marginalization has on individual employees and the group as a whole. We must talk openly with people, one-on-one, to learn about their experiences with bias, and share our own stories to build trust and make the topic safe for discussion. What we discover through those conversations is every bit as important as what shows up in the aggregated data.

An industry colleague, who served as a lead on diversity at a tech company, broke it down for me like this: "When we do our employee surveys, the Latinos always say they are happy. But I'm Latino, and I know that we are often hesitant to rock the boat. Saying the truth is too risky, so we'll say what you want to hear—even if you sit us down in a focus group. I also know that those aggregated numbers where there are enough of us for the $n$ to be significant don't reflect the heterogeneity in our community. Someone who is light-skinned and grew up in Latin America in an upper-middle-class family probably is very happy and comfortable indeed. Someone who is darker-skinned and grew up working-class in America is probably not feeling that same sense of belonging. I'm going to spend time and effort trying to build solutions for the ones I know are at a disadvantage, whether the data tells me that there's a problem with all Latinos or not."

This is a recurring theme. I spoke with 10 diversity and HR professionals at companies with head counts ranging from 60 to 300,000, all of whom are working on programs or interventions for the people who don't register as "big" in big data. They rely at least somewhat on their own intuition when exploring the impact of marginalization. This may seem counter to the mission of people analytics, which is to remove personal perspective and gut feelings from the talent equation entirely. But to discover the effects of bias in our organizations—and to identify complicating factors within groups, such as class and colorism among Latinos and others—we need to collect and analyze qualitative data, too. Intuition can help us find it. The diversity and HR folks described using their "spidey sense" or knowing there is "something in the water"—essentially, understanding that bias is probably a factor, even though people analytics doesn't always prove causes and predict outcomes. Through conversations with employees—and sometimes through focus groups, if the resources are there and participants feel it's safe to be honest—they reality-check what their instincts tell them, often drawing on their own experiences with bias. One colleague said, "The combination of qualitative and quantitative data is ideal, but at the end of the day there is nothing that data will tell us that we don't already know as Black people. I know what my experience was as an African American man who worked for 16 years in roles that weren't related to improving diversity. It's as much heart as head in this work."

## A Call to Action

The proposition at the heart of people analytics is sound—if you want to hire and manage fairly, gut-based decisions are not enough. However, we have to create a new approach, one that also works for small data sets—for the marginalized and the underrepresented.

Here are my recommendations:

First, analysts must challenge the traditional minimum confident $n$, pushing themselves to look beyond the limited hard data. They don't have to prove that the difference in performance ratings between Blacks and whites is "statistically significant" to help managers understand the impact of bias in performance reviews. We already know from the breadth and depth of social science research about bias that it is pervasive in the workplace and influences ratings, so we can combine those insights with what we hear and see on the ground and simply start operating as if bias exists in our companies. We may have to place a higher value on the experiences shared by 5 or 10 employees—or look more carefully at the descriptive data, such as head counts for underrepresented groups and average job satisfaction scores cut by race and gender—to examine the impact of bias at a more granular level.

In addition, analysts should frequently provide confidence intervals—that is, guidance on how much managers can trust the data if the $n$'s are too small to prove statistical significance. When managers get that information, they're more likely to make changes in their hiring and management practices, even if they believe—as most do—that they are already treating people fairly. Suppose, for example, that as Red Ventures began collecting data on self-assessments, analysts had a 75% confidence level that Blacks and Latinos were underrating themselves. The analysts could then have advised managers to go to their minority direct reports, examine the results from that performance period, and determine together whether the self-reviews truly reflected their contributions. It's a simple but collaborative way to address implicit bias or stereotyping that you're reasonably sure is there while giving agency to each employee.

Second, companies also need to be more consistent and comprehensive in their qualitative analysis. Many already conduct interviews and focus groups to gain insights on the challenges of the underrepresented; some even do textual analysis of written performance reviews, exit interview notes, and hiring memos, looking for language that signals bias or negative stereotyping. But we have to go further. We need to find a viable way to create and process more objective performance evaluations, given the internalized biases of both employees and managers, and to determine how those biases affect ratings.

This journey begins with educating all employees on the real-life impact of bias and negative stereotypes. At Facebook we offer a variety of training programs with an emphasis on spotting and counteracting bias, and we keep reinforcing key messages post-training, since we know these muscles take time to build. We issue reminders at critical points to shape decision making and behavior. For example, in our performance evaluation tool, we incorporate prompts for people to check word choice when writing reviews and self-assessments. We remind them, for instance, that terms like "cultural fit" can allow bias to creep in and that they should avoid describing women as "bossy" if they wouldn't describe men who demonstrated the same behaviors that way. We don't yet have data on how this is influencing the language used—it's a new intervention—but we will be examining patterns over time.

Perhaps above all, HR and analytics departments must value both qualitative and quantitative expertise and apply mixed-method approaches everywhere possible. At Facebook we're building cross-functional teams with both types of specialists, because no single research method can fully capture the complex layers of bias that everyone brings to the workplace. We view all research methods as trying to solve the same problem from different angles. Sometimes we approach challenges from a quantitative perspective first, to uncover the "what" before looking to the qualitative experts to dive into the "why" and "how." For instance, if the numbers showed that certain teams were losing or attracting minority employees at higher rates than others (the "what"), we might conduct interviews, run focus groups, or analyze text from company surveys to understand the "why," and pull out themes or lessons for other parts of the company. In other scenarios we might reverse the order of those steps. For example, if we repeatedly heard from members of one social group that they weren't seeing their peers getting recognized at the same rate as people in other groups, we could then investigate whether numerical trends confirmed those observations, or we could conduct statistical analyses to figure out which organizational circumstances were associated with employees' being more or less likely to get recognized.

Cross-functional teams also help us reap the benefits of cognitive diversity. Working together stretches everyone, challenging team members' own assumptions and biases. Getting to absolute "whys" and "hows" on any issue, from recruitment to engagement to performance, is always going to be tough. But we believe that with this approach, we stand the best chance of making improvements across the company. As we analyze the results of Facebook's Pulse survey, given twice a year to employees, and review Performance Summary Cycle inputs, we'll continue to look for signs of problems as well as progress.

## Conclusion

Evidence of discrimination or unfair outcomes may not be as certain or obvious in the workplace as it was for me the time I was evicted from my apartment. But we can increase our certainty, and it's essential that we do so. The underrepresented people at our companies are not crazy to perceive biases working against them, and they can get institutional support.

TAKEAWAYS

Though executives tend to think they're hiring and promoting fairly, bias still creeps into their decisions. People analytics can replace gut decisions with data-driven ones, but firms often say that they don't have enough people from marginalized groups in their data sets to produce reliable insights. Employers can take these steps to supplement small $n$'s and have a better chance of improving diversity and inclusion.

- ✓ Draw on industry data on underrepresented groups, and aggregate your research with reports from other companies in your sector. Extrapolate lessons from similar companies' analyses.

- ✓ Perform textual analysis of written performance reviews, exit interview notes, and hiring memos, looking for language that signals bias or stereotyping.

✓ Get personal—examine individual cases, listen to the experiences of individuals, and use focus groups to gather critical information.

✓ Bring quantitative and qualitative analysis together as you look for signs of problems as well as progress.

*Reprinted from* Harvard Business Review, *November–December 2017 (product #R1706L).*

# Section 2

# HOW YOU CAN MAKE A DIFFERENCE

# HOW TO BE A BETTER ALLY TO YOUR BLACK COLLEAGUES

by Stephanie Creary

T he late singer and songwriter Sam Cooke appropriately summed up the desires of many Black Americans in 1963 when he penned the song, "A Change Is Gonna Come." Well, it's been a long time coming, but corporate America—and the world—has finally woken up to the idea that systemic racism still surrounds us.

As I write this in July 2020, we are in the midst of two interrelated public health crises that have magnified the disparities that Black Americans continue to experience in the United States. More than 130,000 Americans have died from the coronavirus, and the mortality rate for Black Americans has been more than twice as high as that of other U.S. racial groups.[1] Further, our collective witness to the killings of Ahmaud Arbery, George Floyd, Breonna Taylor, Rayshard Brooks, Elijah McClain, and others has called attention to the fact that systemic racism against Black Americans is also a public health crisis. This is not news: We have long known that Black Americans don't have access to adequate educational, health, housing, political, and economic opportunities at the same rates as other racial groups. And, quite simply, the psychological and physiological impact of racism on Black Americans is and has always been devastating.

Yet, it took the collision of these two crises for corporate America to hear that your Black colleagues are not and have never been okay. Now, corporate leaders are calling on their organizations to end systemic racism and support Black employees. While public commitments to antiracism and town hall meetings to discuss race in the workplace have been an important starting point, much more needs to be done to improve the experiences and opportunities of Black employees in corporate America.

## LEAP: A Framework for Becoming a Better Ally to Black Employees

Fourteen years ago, I began studying corporate diversity, equity, and inclusion (DE&I) practices in both the United States and across the world. To date, I have interviewed hundreds of leaders in different sectors and industries about their workplace experiences. My research suggests that the relationship between Black employees and their employing organizations is, at best, a tenuous one. Black employees—at all levels—feel that they have not been adequately heard, understood, or granted opportunities to the same extent as their white peers.

Recently, I developed the LEAP framework, which is designed to help people from different backgrounds build stronger relationships in the workplace. LEAP is based on the idea that relating to people who are different from us takes hard work and can be anxiety-provoking. Yet, doing the necessary work to notice, connect, value, and respond to others' needs results in more effective working relationships.

In this article, I bring together more than a decade's worth of insights on DE&I initiatives and Black employees' experiences and my LEAP framework to propose how company leaders—particularly people managers—who are well-positioned to support Black employees might all LEAP to become better allies in DEI work.

## L: Listen and learn from your Black colleagues' experiences.

Research has shown that Black employees who talk about race, advocate for other Black people, or openly discuss discrimination and unfair treatment at work are penalized for doing so.[2] Yet, when their voices are not suppressed, we learn that Black employees often feel that they have to work harder than their colleagues for the same rewards. In the words of one Black leader:

> I had to be adaptive. I went to a historically Black college and university, so I was not given the same opportunities as those that went to predominantly white colleges and universities. I had to think of different ways of doing things—and doing it a little bit better than those around me to be afforded the same opportunity.

Instead of dampening your Black colleagues' voices and experiences, you can look for opportunities to listen to and learn about their experiences at work. Participating in company-sponsored town halls focused on race in the workplace is one good option. Attending your company's employee resource group (ERG) meetings for Black employees is another.

## E: Engage with Black colleagues in racially diverse and more casual settings.

Since Black employees often feel like they need to overperform at work, gaining deeper insights into their experiences may be more feasible in nonevaluative settings where other Black employees are present. This is echoed in research, which reveals that Black employees are less likely to open up at out-of-the-office social events where they are in the minority but are more likely to share their experiences when they are around other people of color.[3] You may learn that Black colleagues are not getting the support that they need from their direct managers.

Your company's ERG for Black employees is a great place to start. While these groups are specifically designed to address the needs of Black employees, membership and related activities are typically open to all employees from all racial backgrounds.

One Black leader I interviewed explained the significance of his company's Black ERG to his and his colleagues' development:

> *The [ERG] had an impression on me. I had that*
> *early exposure to other Black leaders and saw what*
> *was possible. [The ERG] helps build that pipeline*
> *of the next generation of leaders, which I think for*
> *any company adds real value when you have people*
> *reaching out, being willing to do things above and*
> *beyond the day job to invest in the talent, and to*
> *make sure that there are mechanisms to retain them*
> *if, in fact, they're at risk of leaving the company.*

If your company does not have an ERG for Black employees, consider joining an online community where personal experiences about race are being openly discussed and facilitated by experts.

## A: Ask Black employees about their work and their goals.

Inquiry can be a powerful tool to create connection when people can effectively read social situations and body language. However, when done without care—for example, by focusing on their racial backgrounds, personal lives, or their physical appearance—inquiry can feel overly invasive and harmful to Black workers.

To improve the quality of your relationships with your Black colleagues, ask them about their actual work, including what they are hoping to accomplish, any concerns they have about doing that, and how you might be able to help them reach their vision. One Black leader I spoke with recounted such a conversation:

> *Having [the leader] as a mentor has been significant in my career. We've had a very similar career path. I have been able to talk to him about a lot of the issues that I face. He speaks to me not just in general terms about careers but in specific terms—he offers suggestions based on my experiences. . . . [The relationship has] helped me understand that I need to continually grow and learn.*

Another spoke about a senior leader who encouraged him to advance his education after hearing about his career goals. He said, "You have to work hard to remain competitive in life. Go and take those opportunities."

## P: Provide your Black colleagues with opportunities, suggestions, encouragement, and general support.

It is clear from research from the Center for Talent Innovation and the McKinsey/LeanIn Women in the Workplace report that Black employees often lack the same opportunities at work as their peers from other racial backgrounds.[4] One Black leader in one of my research studies explained her experience and perspective:

> *When I first came into the organization, I didn't get the help that I needed or development that I needed because I was a Black woman, because of stereotypes or people's prejudices or biases. . . . My peers who are minorities who are in the same boat as me have the same issue.*

To support your Black colleagues, amplify their experiences—the good and the bad. Recommend them for highly visible opportunities. Volunteer to provide them with feedback on their work. Introduce them to influential colleagues. Openly acknowledge their accomplishments to others. Reward them for doing DEI work alongside their formal work. And, most of all, share their more challenging experiences with those who have the capacity to create systemic change.

We will only reduce the harmful impact of systemic racism on our Black colleagues when we challenge and change the very structures that create inequality at work, including who we support and how. This will require being more intentional in supporting Black employees, including by asking them first what they need and then supporting them in that way. Your Black colleagues are ready. Are you?

TAKEAWAYS

Black employees feel that they have not been adequately heard, understood, or granted opportunities to the same extent as their white peers. People of different backgrounds—particularly people managers—can become better workplace allies by following these four practices.

✓ Listen and learn from your Black colleagues' experiences. For example, attend your company's employee resource group meetings for Black employees.

✓ Engage with your Black colleagues in racially diverse and casual settings. You may gain deeper insights into their experiences in nonevaluative settings where other Black employees are present.

✓ Ask your Black colleagues about their work and goals. Ask what they are hoping to accomplish, any concerns they have about doing that, and how you might be able to help them reach their vision.

✓ Provide your Black colleagues with opportunities, suggestions, encouragement, and general support. Also, share (anonymously) their more challenging experiences with those who have the capacity to create systemic change.

## NOTES

1. Richard A. Oppel, Jr., Robert Gebeloff, K. K. Rebecca Lai, Will Wright, and Mitch Smith, "The Fullest Look Yet at the Racial Inequity of Coronavirus," *New York Times*, July 5, 2020, https://www.nytimes.com/interactive/2020/07/05/us/coronavirus-latinos-african-americans-cdc-data.html?smtyp=cur&smid=tw-nytimes.

2. Stefanie K. Johnson and David R. Hekman, "Women and Minorities Are Penalized for Promoting Diversity," hbr.org,

March 23, 2016, https://hbr.org/2016/03/women-and-minorities
-are-penalized-for-promoting-diversity.

3. Katherine W. Phillips, Tracy L. Dumas, and Nancy P. Rothbard, "Diversity and Authenticity," *Harvard Business Review*, March–April 2018, https://hbr.org/2018/03/diversity-and-authenticity; Sheryl Estrada, "AT&T Reaches 10-Year Milestone of Celebrating Employee Resource Groups," DiversityInc, November 13, 2018, https://www.diversityinc.com/att-reaches-10-year-milestone-of -celebrating-employee-resource-groups/.

4. Center for Talent Innovation, "Being Black in Corporate America: An Intersectional Exploration," December 9, 2019, https:// www.talentinnovation.org/publication.cfm?publication=1650.

*Adapted from "How to Be a Better Ally to Your Black Colleagues," on hbr.org, July 8, 2020 (product #H05QG9).*

# 7

# HOW THE BEST BOSSES INTERRUPT BIAS ON THEIR TEAMS

by Joan C. Williams and Sky Mihaylo

Companies spend millions on antibias training each year. The goal is to create workforces that are more inclusive, and thereby more innovative and more effective. Studies show that well-managed diverse groups outperform homogeneous ones and are more committed, have higher collective intelligence, and are better at making decisions and solving problems. But research also shows that bias prevention programs rarely deliver.

And some companies don't invest in them at all. So how can you, as an individual leader, make sure your team is including and making the most of diverse voices? Can one person fix what an entire organization can't?

Although bias itself is devilishly hard to eliminate, it is not as difficult to *interrupt*. In the decades we've spent researching and advising people on how to build and manage diverse work groups, we've identified ways that managers can counter bias without spending a lot of time—or political capital.

The first step is to understand the four distinct ways bias plays out in everyday work interactions: (1) *Prove it again:* Some groups have to prove themselves more than others do. (2) *Tightrope:* A narrower range of behaviors is accepted from some groups than from others. (3) *Maternal wall:* Women with children see their commitment and competence questioned or face disapproval for being too career focused. (4) *Tug-of-war:* Disadvantaged groups find themselves pitted against one another because of differing strategies for assimilating—or refusing to do so.

The second step is to recognize when and where these forms of bias arise day-to-day. In the absence of an organizational directive, it's easy to let them go unaddressed. That's a mistake. You can't be a great manager without becoming a *bias interrupter.* Here's how to do it.

# Picking Your People

Bias in hiring has been extensively documented. In one study, "Jamal" needed eight more years of experience than "Greg" to be seen as equally qualified. Another found that men from elite backgrounds were called back for interviews more than 12 times as often as identical candidates from nonelite backgrounds. Other studies have found that women, LGBT+ candidates, people with disabilities, women in headscarves, and older people are less likely to be hired than their peers.

Fairness in hiring is only the first step toward achieving diversity, but it's an important one. Here are four simple actions that will yield the best candidates by eliminating artificial advantages:

## 1. Insist on a diverse pool.

Whether you're working with recruiters or doing the hiring yourself, make it clear from the outset that you want true diversity, not just one female or minority candidate. Research shows that the odds of hiring a woman are 79 times as great if at least two women are in the finalist pool, while the odds of hiring a nonwhite candidate are 194 times as great with at least two finalist minority applicants. For example, when Kori Carew launched the Shook Scholars Institute at Shook, Hardy & Bacon, she designed it to bring a diverse mix of students into the law firm and offered career development and mentoring that prompted many of them to apply for summer associate positions.

## 2. Establish objective criteria, define "culture fit," and demand accountability.

Implicit biases around culture fit often lead to homogeneity. Too often it comes down to shared backgrounds and interests that out-groups, especially first-generation professionals, won't have. That's why it's important to clarify objective criteria for any open role and to rate all applicants using the same rubric. When one insurance company began hiring in this way, it ended up offering jobs to 46% more minority candidates than before. Even if your organization doesn't mandate this approach, ensure that everyone on your team uses it. Write down the specific qualifications required for a particular position so that everyone can focus on them when reviewing résumés and conducting interviews. For example, when

Alicia Powell was managing chief counsel at PNC Bank, she made a point of listing the qualities that would make new team members successful in their roles: proactive in managing risk, self-disciplined, patient, customer focused, and independent. Powell shared this information with the rest of her team and candidates, ensuring that everyone was on the same page. You should hold people accountable in the same way. Waive criteria rarely, and require an explanation for those exceptions; then keep track of long-term waiving trends. Research shows that objective rules tend to be applied rigorously to out-groups but leniently to in-groups.

## 3. Limit referral hiring.

If your organization is homogeneous, hiring from within or from employees' social networks will only perpetuate that. So reach out to women and minority groups. Google partners with historically Black colleges such as Spelman and Florida A&M University and with Hispanic-serving institutions such as New Mexico State and the University of Puerto Rico, Mayagüez. As an individual leader, you can work with the same organizations or recruit from similar ones in your industry or local community.

# 4. Structure interviews with skills-based questions.

Ask every person interviewed the same questions, and make sure that each question directly relates to the desired knowledge and skills you've outlined. Rate the answers immediately—that will allow you to compare candidates fairly on a preestablished rubric and prevent favoritism. You should also use skills assessments: Rather than ask, "How comfortable are you with Excel?" say, "Here's a data set. How would you find out $X$?" For more-complex skills, such as project management, pose a problem or a task that candidates are likely to encounter on the job, and ask them to describe in detail how they would handle it.

## Managing Day-to-Day

Even good leaders sometimes fall into bad habits when it comes to the daily management of their teams. Women report doing about 20% more "office housework," on average, than their white male counterparts, whether it's literal housework (arranging for lunch or cleaning up after a meeting), administrative tasks (finding a place to meet or prepping a PowerPoint), emotional labor ("He's upset—can you fix it?"), or undervalued work (mentoring summer interns). This is especially true in high-status, high-stakes workplaces. Women engineers report a "worker bee" expectation at higher rates than white men do, and women of color report it at higher rates than white women do. Meanwhile, glamour work that leads to networking and promotion opportunities, such as project leadership and presentations, goes disproportionately to white men. When the consultancy GapJumpers analyzed the performance reviews of a tech company client, it found that women employees were 42% more likely than their male colleagues to be limited to lower-impact projects; as a result, far fewer of them rose to more-senior roles.

Meetings are another problem area. Research shows that men are more likely than women to dominate the conversation, and that whereas men with expertise tend to be *more* influential, women with expertise tend to be *less* so. Our study of lawyers found that half of women report being interrupted in meetings at a higher rate than their male peers are. Another study found that in meetings that included more men than women (a common scenario), women typically participated about 25% less often than their male coworkers did. Double standards and stereotypes play out whenever diverse identities come together. Is a woman "emotional," or a Black man "angry," while a white male is "passionate"? We once heard from a woman scientist that she was sharply criticized as "aggressive" when she brought up a flaw in a male colleague's analysis; after that she felt she needed to just "bring in baked goods and be agreeable." A Black tech company executive we know told us about a meeting during which she said little while the only other woman, an Asian American, said a lot. But she later heard that people thought she had "dominated" the conversation while her Asian American peer had been "very quiet."

Unsure whether this sort of thing is happening on your team? Start tracking assignments and airtime in meetings. Use our free online tools (available at https://biasinterrupters.org/toolkits/orgtools/) to find out which work done by your group is higher- or lower-profile and who's doing what. For meetings, pay attention: Who's at the table? Who's doing the talking? Is someone taking notes when he or she could be leading the conversation? If you find a problematic dynamic, here are some ways to change it:

## 1. Set up a rotation for office housework, and don't ask for volunteers.

"I always give these tasks to women because they do them well/volunteer" is a common refrain. This dynamic reflects an environment in which men suffer few consequences for bypassing or doing a poor job on low-value work, while women who do the same are seen as "prima donnas" or incompetent. Particularly when administrative staff is limited, a rotation helps level the playing field and makes it clear that everyone is expected to contribute to office housework. If you ask for volunteers, women and people of color will feel powerful pressure to prove they are "team players" by raising their hands.

## 2. Mindfully design and assign people to high-value projects.

Sometimes we hear "It's true, I keep giving the plum assignments to a small group—but they're the only ones with the skills to do them!" According to Joyce Norcini, formerly general counsel for Nokia Siemens Networks, if you have only a tight circle of people you trust to handle meaningful work, you're in trouble. Her advice: Reconsider who is capable of doing what these important jobs require; chances are someone not on your usual list is. You may need to move outside your comfort zone and be more involved in the beginning, but having a broader range of trained people will serve you well in the end.

## 3. Acknowledge the importance of lower-profile contributions.

"Diversity" hires may lag behind their majority-member peers because they're doing extra stuff that doesn't get them extra credit. If your organization truly prioritizes inclusion, then walk your talk. Many bosses who say they value diversity programming and mentorship don't actually take it into account when promotion or comp time becomes available. Integrating these contributions into individual goal setting and evaluating them during performance reviews is a simple start. And don't be afraid to think big: A law partner we know did such a great job running the woman's initiative that the firm begged her to stay on for another year. She said she would if the firm's bosses made her an equity partner. They did.

## 4. Respond to double standards, stereotyping, "manterruption," "bropriating," and "whipeating."

Pay close attention to the way people on your team talk about their peers and how they behave in group settings. For example, men tend to interrupt women far more often than the other way around; displays of confidence and directness *decrease* women's influence but *increase* men's. If a few people are dominating the conversation in a meeting, address it directly. Create and enforce a policy for interruptions. Keep track of those who drown others out and talk with them privately about it, explaining that you think it's important to hear everyone's contributions. Similarly, when you see instances of "bropriating" or "whipeating"—that is, majority-group members taking or being given credit for ideas that women and people of color originally offered—call it out. We know two women on the board of directors of a public company who made a pact: When a man tried to claim one of their ideas, the other would say something like, "Yes, I liked Sandra's point, and I'm glad you did too." Once they did this consistently, bropriating stopped.

## 5. Ask people to weigh in.

Women, people of Asian descent, and first-generation professionals report being brought up with a "modesty mandate" that can lead them to hold back their thoughts or speak in a tentative, deferential way. Counter this by extending an invitation: "Camilla, you have experience with this—what are we missing? Is this the best course of action?"

## 6. Schedule meetings inclusively.

Business meetings should take place in the office, not at a golf course, a university club, or your favorite concert venue. Otherwise you're giving an artificial advantage to people who feel more comfortable in those settings or whose personal interests overlap with yours. Whenever possible, stick to working hours, or you risk putting caregivers and others with a demanding personal life at a disadvantage. Joan once noticed that no mothers were participating in a faculty appointment process because all the meetings were held at 5:30 p.m. When she pointed this out to the person leading them, the problem was fixed immediately. This colleague had a stay-at-home wife and simply hadn't thought about the issue before.

## 7. Equalize access proactively.

Bosses may meet with some employees more regularly than others, but it's important to make sure this is driven by business demands and team needs rather than by what individuals want or expect. White men may feel more comfortable walking into your office or asking for time. The same may be true of people whose interests you share. When Emily Gould Sullivan, who has led the employment law functions for two *Fortune* 500 retail companies, realized that she was routinely accepting "walking meeting" invitations from a team member who was, like her, interested in fitness, she made a point of reaching out to others to equalize access.

## Developing Your Team

Your job as a manager is not only to get the best performance out of your team but also to encourage the development of each member. That means giving fair performance reviews, equal access to high-potential assignments, and promotions and pay increases to those who have earned them. Unfortunately, as we've noted, some groups need to prove themselves more than others, and a broader range of behaviors is often accepted from white men. For example, our research shows that assertiveness and anger are less likely to be accepted from people of color, and expectations that women will be modest, self-effacing, and nice often affect performance assessments. One study found that 66% of women's reviews contained comments about their personalities, but only 1% of men's reviews did. These double standards can have a real impact on equity outcomes. PayScale found that men of color were 25% less likely than their white peers to get a raise when they asked for one. And gender norms stunt careers for women. PayScale found that when women and men start their careers on the same rung of the professional ladder, by the time they are halfway (aged 30–44), 47% of men are managers or higher, but only 40% of women are. These numbers just worsen over time: Only 3% of the women make it to the C-suite, compared with 8% of the men.

Take these steps to avoid common pitfalls in evaluations and promotions:

## 1. Clarify evaluation criteria and focus on performance, not potential.

Don't arrive at a rating without thinking about what predetermined benchmarks you've used to get there. Any evaluation should include enough data for a third party to understand the justification for the rating. Be specific. Instead of, "She writes well," say, "She can write an effective summary judgment motion under a tight deadline."

## 2. Separate performance from potential and personality from skill sets.

In-groups tend to be judged on their potential and given the benefit of the doubt, whereas out-groups have to show they've nailed it. If your company values potential, it should be assessed separately, with factors clearly outlined for evaluators and employees. Then track whether there's a pattern as to who has "potential." If so, try relying on performance alone for everyone, or get even more concrete with what you're measuring. Personality comments are no different; be wary of double standards that affect women and people of color when it comes to showing emotion or being congenial. Policing women into femininity doesn't help anyone, and—as courts have pointed out—it's direct evidence of sex discrimination. If that's not motivation enough, evaluators can miss critical skills by focusing on personality. It's more valuable, and accurate, to say someone is a strong collaborator who can manage projects across multiple departments than to say, "She's friendly and gets along with everyone."

## 3. Level the playing field with respect to self-promotion.

The modesty mandate mentioned above prevents many people in out-groups from writing effective self-evaluations or defending themselves at review time. Counter that by giving everyone you manage the tools to evaluate their own performance. Be clear that it's acceptable, and even expected, to advocate for oneself. A simple two-pager can help overcome the modesty mandate and cue majority men (who tend toward overconfidence) to provide concrete evidence for their claims.

## 4. Explain how training, promotion, and pay decisions will be made, and follow those rules.

As the chair of her firm's women's initiative, one lawyer we know developed a strategy to ensure that all candidates for promotion were considered fairly. She started with a clear outline of what was needed to advance and then assigned every eligible employee (already anonymized) to one of three groups: green (meets the objective metrics), yellow (is close), and red (doesn't). Then she presented the color-coded list to the rest of the evaluation team. By anonymizing the data and pregrouping the candidates by competencies, she ensured that no one was forgotten or recommended owing to in-group favoritism.

All the evaluators were forced to stick to the predetermined benchmarks, and as a result, they tapped the best candidates. (Those in the yellow category were given advice about how to move up to green.) When it comes to promotions, there may be limits to what you can do as an individual manager, but you should push for transparency on the criteria used. When they are explicit, it's harder to bend the rules for in-group members.

## Conclusion

Organizational change is crucial, but it doesn't happen overnight. Fortunately, you can begin with all these recommendations *today*.

Companies spend millions on antibias training each year in hopes of creating more-inclusive workforces, but these programs rarely deliver. Although bias itself is devilishly hard to change, it is not as difficult to interrupt. There are several practices that individual managers can use to counter bias as part of their everyday work.

- ✓ In hiring, leaders should insist on a diverse pool, precommit to objective criteria, limit referral hiring, and structure interviews around skills-based questions.

- ✓ Day to day, they should ensure that high- and low-value work is assigned evenly and run meetings in a way that guarantees all voices are heard.

- ✓ In evaluating and developing people, they should clarify criteria for positive reviews and promotions, stick to those rules, and separate potential from performance and personality from skill sets.

*Reprinted from* Harvard Business Review, *November–December 2019 (product #R1906L).*

# 8

# HOW TO CALL OUT RACIAL INJUSTICE AT WORK

by James R. Detert and Laura Morgan Roberts

I n this time of intense pain, anger, and collective attention, many people—African Americans especially—
are seizing the moment to speak truth to power at
work. They are holding senior leaders accountable for
their commitments to increased diversity, confronting
colleagues or clients who make insensitive or ignorant
comments, and calling out those who mock the Black
Lives Matter movement or dismiss calls for justice and
human rights.

Speaking up in this way is risky, but studies beyond the realm of conversations about race have shown that it is also vitally important. It's key to our individual and collective well-being, learning, and ultimately organizational performance.[1]

We desperately need people to be courageous enough to undertake these actions. So how can you take a stand for advancing racial justice in your own organization in a way that improves your chances for leading change from within, mitigates risk of rejection, and preserves your career options and mental health?

Speaking up about hard truths at work is difficult for just about everyone, especially about issues that in some way implicate those above us. We fear—for good reason—that we'll suffer career, social, psychological, or other kinds of harm for being honest about difficult issues.[2] When those issues directly implicate people's integrity, the risks of an in-the-moment explosion or after-the-fact consequence only escalate. Thus, people who champion diversity face a host of negative consequences because of widespread resistance toward targeted efforts to promote equity and inclusion.

As high as these stakes are for white people who speak up, they're higher if you're Black. Raise these issues and you risk being seen as biased, overly emotional (too angry, for example), and a host of other negative stereotypes that lie beyond the problems you're trying to get addressed.[3]

Here's an insidious example from one of us (Jim): In one of my classes I present students with a story of a Black manager being called a racial slur by a white subordinate and ask what the Black boss should do. Students typically advise that the manager should turn to HR for help so he won't be seen as unfair in his discipline of a white subordinate. Asked what they would tell the manager if he were white, some of those same students typically see him as capable of taking disciplinary action against a subordinate of any race without help.

Courageous actions are rooted in people's willingness to sacrifice their security and stability for the sake of a cause that is greater than their career advancement. But that doesn't mean that you should be cavalier about raising issues of racial justice. Our research has shown that there are ways to approach this work that mitigate your risk of being derailed or dismissed—and give you the best chance of being heard.[4] Here are five strategies to help you maximize the impact of your courageous acts when speaking truth to power at work:

## Use Allies and Speak as a Collective

Find like-minded colleagues and raise the issue together. People we studied reported that speaking up as a group on workplace issues had more of an impact because it was hard to write them off as "one disgruntled person."[5] Collective voice is especially impactful when it comes from a multicultural coalition of allies. It's harder to dismiss non-Black allies on the grounds of being biased or self-interested, and a unified voice shows that Black issues are *human*. If you can't find a group within your company, use social proof by pointing to others (ideally whose view the person you're speaking to respects or cares about) who share your point of view.

Examples of groups that have applied collective pressure for antiracist institutional changes include Google employees, who filed a petition demanding that the company stop selling software to police units, and members of Kansas State's college football team, who refused to play until the school met their demands for demonstrating accountability for racist actions on campus.

## Channel Your Emotions (But Don't Suppress Them!)

Revealing the full extent of your rage or despair in front of those with power sets you up to be dismissed or punished for being "too emotional." It's completely justifiable to be angry (outraged!), hurt, and sad about the things we've witnessed time and again. (We are too!) And you shouldn't ignore these emotions: Find safe spaces to help you to honor them, so that you can channel them as energy that fuels your next steps—conversations with confidantes, for example, or with counselors. Then, after you are feeling centered, you might call attention to the racial injustice that occurred.

Here's an example: Terrence, a young Black man, confronted his significantly older, white boss about using racial slurs at work. It was a bold move for Terrence to call out this behavior in public given the hierarchical nature of the place and the knowledge that there were "a lot of racist people working there in higher positions." Despite the strong emotions he felt, Terrence spoke in a firm and measured way, showing compassion and a desire to help correct rather than shame or scold his boss. This allowed his boss to see the ignorance and hurtfulness of his statements and, according to one of Terrence's colleagues, led him to change his ways, rather than reacting defensively.

## Anticipate Others' Negative Reactions

As much as this feels like a time to focus on your own feelings of outrage and pain, you should also anticipate strong emotional reactions from the people you're confronting. Demanding improvements in racial equity stands a good chance of evoking defensiveness and fear. Inquiry and framing can help to defuse negative reactions and align shared goals.

For example, if your request evokes a furrowed brow or a crossing of arms across the chest, start asking questions: "These seem like appropriate next steps to me, but perhaps they feel problematic to you. Can you help me understand what you're thinking, and why these may not seem right to you?" You don't have to agree with what gets said next, but your effort to acknowledge that your counterpart has feelings too can increase your chance of reaching a mutually satisfactory outcome.

## Frame What You Say So That It's Compelling to Your Counterpart

Delivering your message as inclusively as possible can help with the sense of divisiveness often associated with calls for racial justice. Make it easier for those you're imploring to change to see your message as coming from a position of "we are evolving together" rather than "I am revolting against you." This framing highlights collective progress, which—even when modest—helps people to cultivate positive identities and to find meaning and persistence on challenging projects at work.[6] If possible, make note of at least one way your organization has already made progress on racial inclusion (such as a town hall Q&A, public statement, task forces, investing in minority business enterprises), and try to build from there.

When you're trying to compel others to act differently, especially those above you, it's also critical to use language that will resonate with them, rather than the arguments that are meaningful only to you. When advocating for change, for instance, many of us often lead with economic or instrumental arguments. However, in this case that's not a tenable option. Arguing for racial equity on the sole basis of financial gain suggests that basic justice and decency toward people of all races is optional unless it can be proven to have some economic value. It's not optional, and requiring people of color to justify their demands for basic human rights in this degrading manner is yet another injury inflicted on them.

You can reframe this moral imperative in a way that resonates with your audience, however. If, for example, your boss is motivated by external threats, explain how your proposals will keep customers who are disgusted by your company's lack of action from abandoning you. If your boss is more excited by opportunities, talk about how embracing this moral imperative will attract customers and top talent.

## Follow Up

After a difficult conversation, often the last thing we want to do is to reengage anytime soon. But no matter how well you handled yourself in the first encounter, these topics are so sensitive that there's a decent chance someone you talked to left the discussion feeling personally indicted or that you felt misunderstood. If you need those people to stand with you for real change to take root, you'll want to check in.

Start by acknowledging the difficulty of the subject: "I know our conversation was a really tough one, and I imagine it could have left you with lingering feelings. Can we talk about that?" That can be a powerful way to move forward together, and it also gives you the opportunity to clarify misunderstandings and to nail down details like resource commitments, action steps, and agreements on measurement and accountability that can give your call for change a better chance of real success.

Our aim in providing this advice is not to place an additional burden on people of color, who already must deal with the unfair weight of their counterparts' hurt feelings even as they themselves are targets of injustice. Instead we acknowledge the reality of those burdens and the unfairness of that racial work and hope to give people of color and their allies greater agency, discretion, and impact during this historic moment of change. In so doing, we also aim to lessen the repercussions of speaking out about racial injustice for people's well-being and careers.

A final thought about the courage it takes to speak up in the workplace about racial injustice: If you have attempted to implement these suggestions and still see little to no progress, take stock of where you are and where you wish to be. It might be time to look around your organization for a new team or assignment with leaders and allies who are willing to join you in this work. Or it might be time for you to find a new organization where you employ your talents among those more demonstrably committed to the changes you seek.

TAKEAWAYS

It takes courage to speak up about racial injustice at work, and raising these issues brings risk, especially for Black employees. However, there are five strategies you can use to improve your chances for leading change from within, mitigating risk of rejection, and preserving your career options and mental health.

- ✓ Use allies to speak as a collective. Find like-minded colleagues and raise the issue together.

- ✓ Channel your emotions (but don't suppress them). Revealing the full extent of your rage or despair sets you up to be treated dismissively.

- ✓ Anticipate others' negative reactions. Speaking up may evoke defensiveness and fear.

- ✓ Frame what you say so it's compelling to your counterpart. Make it easier for those you're imploring to change to see your message as coming from a position of "we are evolving together."

- ✓ Follow up afterward. If you need people to stand with you for real change to take root, you'll want to check in.

## NOTES

1. Timothy D. Maynes and Philip M. Podsakoff, "Speaking More Broadly: An Examination of the Nature, Antecedents, and Consequences of an Expanded Set of Employee Voice Behaviors," *Journal of Applied Psychology* 99, no. 1 (January 2014): https://pubmed.ncbi.nlm.nih.gov/24041119/; and James R. Detert, Ethan R.

Burris, David A. Harrison, and Sean R. Martin, "Voice Flows to and Around Leaders: Understanding When Units Are Helped or Hurt by Employee Voice," *Administrative Science Quarterly* 58, no. 4 (October 17, 2013): https://journals.sagepub.com/doi/10.1177/0001839213510151.

2. James R. Detert and Evan A. Bruno, "Workplace Courage: Review, Synthesis, and Future Agenda for a Complex Construct," *Academy of Management Annals* 11, no. 2 (March 15, 2017): https://psycnet.apa.org/record/2018-15086-002.

3. Adia Harvey Wingfield, "Are Some Emotions Marked 'Whites Only'? Racialized Feeling Rules in Professional Workplaces," *Social Problems* 57, no. 2 (May 1, 2010): https://academic.oup.com/socpro/article-abstract/57/2/251/1655563.

4. James R. Detert, "Cultivating Everyday Courage," *Harvard Business Review*, November–December 2018, https://hbr.org/2018/11/cultivating-everyday-courage.

5. Detert, "Cultivating Everyday Courage."

6. Jane E. Dutton, Laura Morgan Roberts, and Jeffrey Bednar, "Pathways for Positive Identity Construction at Work: Four Types of Positive Identity and the Building of Social Resources," *Academy of Management Review* 35, no. 2 (April 2010): https://journals.aom.org/doi/abs/10.5465/amr.35.2.zok265.

*Adapted from "How to Call Out Racial Injustice at Work," on hbr.org, July 16, 2020 (product #H05QRG).*

# About the Contributors

**STEPHANIE CREARY** is an assistant professor at the University of Pennsylvania's Wharton School of Management.

**JAMES R. DETERT** is a professor of business administration and the associate dean of executive degree programs and leadership initiatives at the University of Virginia's Darden School of Business.

**MARK R. KRAMER** is a senior lecturer at Harvard Business School and a cofounder and a managing director of FSG, a global social-impact consulting firm.

**ROBERT W. LIVINGSTON** is the author of *The Conversation: How Seeking and Speaking the Truth About Racism Can Radically Transform Individuals and Organizations*. He also serves on the faculty of the Harvard Kennedy School.

**ANTHONY J. MAYO** is the Thomas S. Murphy Senior Lecturer of Business Administration in the organizational behavior unit of Harvard Business School.

**SKY MIHAYLO** is the Policy and Research Fellow at the Center for WorkLife Law at the University of California's Hastings College of the Law.

**LAURA MORGAN ROBERTS** is a professor of practice at the University of Virginia's Darden School of Business and the coeditor of *Race, Work, and Leadership: New Perspectives on the Black Experience* (Harvard Business Review Press, 2019).

**ELLA F. WASHINGTON** is a professor of practice at Georgetown University's McDonough School of Business and the founder of Ellavate Solutions, which provides executive coaching and diversity and inclusion strategy and training for organizations.

**JAMES D. WHITE** is the former chairman, president, and CEO of Jamba Juice. White has also held leadership positions at Safeway Stores, the Gillette Company, Nestlé-Purina, and Coca-Cola. White also sits on several corporate boards, including those of Medallia, Panera Bread, and Simply Good Food.

**JOAN C. WILLIAMS** is a professor and the founding director of the Center for WorkLife Law at the University of California's Hastings College of the Law. Her newest book is

*White Working Class: Overcoming Class Cluelessness in America* (Harvard Business Review Press, 2017).

**MAXINE WILLIAMS** is Facebook's global chief diversity officer.

# Index

# Is Your Business Ready for the Future?

If you enjoyed this book and want more on today's pressing business topics, turn to other books in the **Insights You Need** series from *Harvard Business Review*. Featuring HBR's latest thinking on topics critical to your company's success—from Blockchain and Cybersecurity to AI and Agile—each book will help you explore these trends and how they will impact you and your business in the future.

**FOR MORE VISIT HBR.ORG/BOOKS**